THE ORPHANED GENERATION

*Estrangement Between
Parents and Adult Children*

by

June Ann Elston

Just like a beautiful flower
slowly shedding its petals until nothing is left,
so too an estranged family.

Dedication

To all families estranged
from adult children
and
especially to those families
who participated
anonymously
in this book

How sharper than a serpent's tooth it is to have a thankless child.

--Shakespeare

Acknowledgements

I would like to thank my editor, Phyllis Dolislager, who unexpectedly came into my life with more than a talent for editing. There is a serenity about her that helped keep my focus on the completion of this book.

I am grateful to my dear friends Jean Clarke and Ronnie Marx for their early and constant support for this book.

I can never adequately thank my husband, Roger, for his continued encouragement and endless love.

CONTENTS

Introduction

Because of the dreadful circumstances surrounding my great loss of family, I decided to take pen and paper (the old fashioned way), not the computer, and write my story—just for myself. I thought it might be therapeutic and that it might help me understand what had happened.

It took a long time to complete. When I was done, I chose to share my story with a close friend, who was witness to some of the horror of my family loss. In our many conversations, over time, I found myself questioning the probability of estrangement happening in other families. What if other families were harboring this same ugly secret of estrangement from their adult children? What if they felt ashamed to admit they had lost contact with their adult children? What if those families wanted to share their stories? Maybe they needed a platform to do it. The big question was WHY?? Why would they want to share their painful stories?

A theory began to tickle my brain—the reason for this book—to provoke a national conversation about this epidemic. A subject as sensitive as this should be getting a great deal more attention. The reason these families might be willing to tell their stories would be to inform other families experiencing the same sadness that they are not alone. It might empower them to be stronger.

I decided to experiment and test my theory by placing ads in the local newspapers. I invited people to share their family stories, anonymously with me, for a book I hoped to write. To my surprise, I received a number of responses from families more than willing to tell their stories. This book is a compilation of stories of parents estranged from their adult children that may at times shock you, may make you cry, or even depress you. These people could be your neighbors, or even your friends, who were never able to share their sad stories with people they know.

This book is about families whose children did not suffer abuse, deprivation or neglect. In fact, from my interviews, the children were very well cared for. Why then the estrangement? I thought I might find a common thread running through the stories. I imagined some theories, although far from scientific. In some cases, divorce, money issues — parents excessively accommodating their kids without any expectation of responsibility — and parents too controlling.

The biggest surprise was that in many cases it was not any of the above, but rather what I have come to call, "Mind Control" by the in-laws — son-in-law, daughter-in-law and in-laws (parents-in-law). The in-laws were changing the family dynamics by slowly cutting off all contact.

However, emerging from this theory is the question, how much responsibility do the adult children have in abandoning their parents? In some cases, the integrity of the family is broken by the reluctance of the in-laws to include the parents, but not without the adult child's acquiescence. What are these children made of? Are there character flaws in them? Are they too weak to stand up against the alienation of their parents and a way of life which should include them? Is this a new age of "disposable parents", like diapers?

Many therapists believe parents should never give up hope of reconciliation with their children. I don't agree with that theory, although I am not a professional. I only have my personal non-scientific opinion.

I believe there is "HOPE" and "FALSE HOPE". I don't believe "Hope" should be open-ended. In order to go through the stages of emotional upheaval because of estrangement from adult children and reach a place of acceptance, there has to be a cut-off of "False Hope" in order to heal. How much time has to elapse before one decides to stop "hoping" and move on to a healthier place? It becomes a personal choice. No one can tell another "it's time to move forward." It is apparent to some that this generation of adult children is an unforgiving one.

This book may give you some insight into the tragedy of losing a child WHO IS STILL ALIVE.

The word "orphan" means a child whose parents are dead. The word "orphan" has never been used to describe parents abandoned by their adult children, who "consider" their parents to be dead.

Perhaps, because we parents grew up in a more authoritative environment than our adult children, it would never occur to us to abandon our parents, no matter 'the crime'. Therefore, we are now the "Orphaned Generation".

This ad was placed in five different newspapers over a period of two years. Most of the stories in this book came from responses to this ad.

*   *   *

6 STAGES OF EMOTION ESTRANGED PARENTS EXPERIENCE

1. SHOCK   confusion and disbelief

2. GUILT   must have done or said
                    something terrible to trigger
                    this reaction

3. REPAIR   telephone, email, letters of
                    apology

4. ANGER   ungrateful, unrelenting, never
                    told us what is wrong

5. ACCEPTANCE   tried working to change
                    situation. Did nothing to
                    cause life-changing family
                    dynamics

6. SADNESS   great, overwhelming

*Peace can only come when one stops expecting —
and starts accepting.*

The Holidays

I would be remiss if I didn't address the challenges facing us at times when most families are celebrating holidays. I lump all holidays together—religious and secular. I separate only one from the rest—Mother's Day!! I believe it deserves special commentary.

Using Thanksgiving as an example, I found that a certain rhythm settles in after many years of having the holidays at my home. Part of that celebration begins as early as making the list of ingredients for all the recipes, the buying and preparing of them, washing the dishes, setting the table, etc. Sharing these chores with the children extends the pleasure of the holiday, instead of just sharing the dinner itself. It is one of those precious moments of a special family holiday.

When it is all taken away because our children have chosen to 'divorce' us, what are we left with? Painful memories of what we had and what we have lost . . . an empty holiday. When this first occurred, I tried ignoring the holiday—it did not work. I tried eating in restaurants with friends. It did not work. Thru trial and error, I found celebrating Thanksgiving at my home and inviting friends and neighbors, who were alone, made the holiday special for them, and that worked for me.

Mother's Day

Mother's day is a challenge different from all other holidays. It celebrates being a mom, which we no longer are in our 'lost' children's eyes. No other holiday carries the pain of loss to such an extreme degree. It is the most painful for mothers estranged from their children.

Coping with the emptiness of this holiday is different for each of us. I have tried not seeing anyone, being very busy with friends, changing my routines. For me, there is no one thing to try, but a few different things. Perhaps these suggestions might give you food for thought.

Find one thing that is different from anything you have done before. Find that one thing that brings you a little joy, take a deep breath, and enjoy something nature has to offer. The most difficult: make a list of some good things in your life and be grateful for them.

The following pages contain stories of families who are experiencing "the orphaned generation" estrangement.

ONE

Children, Reputation, Money . . . All Gone

I was 75 years old when I found out I was in debt for over one million dollars and would have to file bankruptcy immediately.

It had all started a few years before. My son-in-law Alan was in a retail furniture business with a partner he was not happy with. Alan wanted to open his own furniture store and close the one he was in. He asked me to help him out by using my name as president of the corporation he wanted to create. He also wanted to use my American Express card. I stupidly agreed. Alan found a location for the new store, made his contacts with suppliers, and opened the store using my name and my credit for everything.

Then I got a frantic call from my daughter, Jenny, screaming that something had gone terribly wrong at the first store, and they needed immediate cash — a lot of cash. They had no money for food and necessary every day expenses.

At that time, I only had a retirement account worth about $75,000.00 and a CD worth $45,000.00. I immediately took a loan out against my CD and had the bank wire them the money. I cashed in $30,000.00 of my retirement account and sent that too. Alan liquidated the first store, and to this day I have never found out what actually happened

Alan started making sales in the new store and agreed to start paying off my CD loan. He also agreed to pay a small amount toward my retirement account. For a few years during this period of growth, my daughter Jenny and son-in-law were buying new homes and new cars. And then the bubble burst. No more stores, no more income, only big debts. Of course, I was the one financially responsible, even though I never had anything to do with running the business. I was just trying to help my children. The CD loan I had taken out was not fully repaid, and my retirement account was never replaced.

When I finally filed bankruptcy, to my dismay, I learned that it did not discharge any sales tax that the corporation might owe.

My granddaughter Ann was twelve and studying for her Bat Mitzvah (coming of age in Judaism) when my daughter filed for divorce. It was a very stressful time for them, especially since my son-in-law Alan had found someone else.

For the most part, I enjoyed a close relationship with my daughter Jenny although at times it was somewhat contentious. I started to notice a change in my daughter's behavior towards me soon after I remarried, as my husband had died the year before. Living across the country from each other, our contact was almost daily by telephone. The phone calls became fewer, and her attitude started to grow quite hostile. I chalked it up to the stress of her divorce: an ex-husband planning to remarry, no one special in her life, and the planning of a Bat Mitzvah for all parties to share a milestone in her daughter's life.

As the time approached for the Bat Mitzvah, my daughter's behavior seemed to grow more out of control. Then I received a notice that there was $50,000.00 due on state taxes that my son-in-law had never paid, and technically was not responsible for. I was responsible because I was still the president of his corporation. Just when I thought I could put the nightmare behind me, it came back to haunt me again.

My daughter was adamant that I should talk to my ex-son-in-law and his whole family at Ann's Bat Mitzvah. It became a great big obstacle towards sharing a special day for Ann — one that we had all looked forward to. My daughter had made up her mind that I was going to ruin this special day because I told her that I would not speak to my son-in-law or his family. I showed her the delinquent tax bill I had received from the state for $50,000.00, that was never paid by my son-in-law and was due immediately — and once again my responsibility. That made fifty thousand reasons why I would never talk to him. But I finally agreed to talk to his family and girlfriend at the Bat Mitzvah.

We arrived at the Synagogue, and I immediately went to the ladies room, passing everyone in the lobby so that I could get up the courage to face Alan and his family. My daughter followed me and proceeded to have the worst meltdown I have ever experienced. I could not calm her down, and she did not want to listen to my explanation. I was willing to talk to everyone, except my-son-law. It was a terrible scene, and everyone in the lobby heard it. I was humiliated further when my part in the religious service was taken away from me at the last minute and given to someone else. That was the last time my daughter ever spoke to me.

Another mistake I made, among many, was going back to my daughter's house, after the celebration. I should have gone to a hotel. However, I was concerned about my granddaughter not understanding. When we got back to my daughter's house, I tried to explain some of it to my granddaughter. It was an impossible task because Ann had no knowledge of the damage her father had caused in so many lives. I did however, read the prepared speech that I was supposed to have read to Ann, at the Bat Mitzvah, in the privacy of her room.

With all the mistakes I made through the years, I could never get past the fact that I not only gave my daughter most of my money (little that I had) but also my good name. My reputation was more important than the money. I was well past my prime, and could not replace the great loss.

I sent emails to my granddaughter and received horrendous ranting emails from my daughter. I finally received an email from Ann, my granddaughter, telling me not to write anymore unless I was prepared to apologize to her mother. I could not do that. Subsequently on the Jewish New Year, I wrote to Ann explaining that forgiveness was part of the celebration and hoped we could move on. I also started sending emails once a month. This continued for a couple of years, and I eventually received an email telling me not to write anymore.

My granddaughter recently celebrated her 16th birthday. I decided to send her a special gift through a family friend. It was rejected. Sad to say, that was the last time there was any communication between us.

TWO

Military—The Ultimate Way of Life

My wife Rachel and I have been married for 50 years. We were married very young, just 21 years old. We had a very normal family life. We had three children, two girls and a boy. We were very close and took our children wherever we went, including family vacations.

My older daughter Lori got married first. She met her husband at college. She brought him home, and although we were disappointed in her choice, we never said anything. Sam was of Arab descent and culturally different from Lori. The difference didn't seem to matter to Lori, and Sam fooled us into believing he only wanted to make her happy. Sam was in the military and stationed at Ft. Bragg. He was part of an elite military special forces.

They decided to marry, and we made a beautiful wedding for them. We became friends with Sam's family. We were invited to Sam's two brothers' weddings, and our families enjoyed special occasions together.

Lori gave birth to a baby boy, Michael, and we were thrilled even though they were in North Carolina and we were in New York. We made a few trips to visit them and naturally as grandparents will do, we brought gifts for the baby. We started to notice a change in attitude with Lori. Something was bothering her. My wife would ask what the problem was and was told 'nothing is wrong'. This went on and happened whether we were visiting them or they visited us.

Finally, one Saturday night, I decided to call Lori in the hope she would tell me what was bothering her. My son-in-law, Sam answered the phone and became quite nasty. When I asked to talk to Lori, he hung up on me. I called back, and Lori answered the phone. I tried to talk to her, and she said "Have a nice life," and hung up. That was the last time I talked to Lori. My other daughter Connie and my son David tried calling them. Sam told David that we were undermining his authority by bringing gifts to the baby against their wishes.

Lori wiped out the whole family, refusing to even talk to her grandmother, who she had been very close to. After the blowup, I called Sam's parents to see what help they could be. Sam's mother had no say in anything in their life. His father was the master of the family, as in many Arab cultures. They knew we were decent people and loved the children, yet they refused to help mediate the situation.

The children moved from North Carolina to New Jersey. Time passed and we still could not see our grandson. We decided to seek legal help. We were told that the best scenario would be a court order allowing "supervised visitation". We decided to drop that idea as it would be too painful, and too destructive to our grandson, Michael.

Years went by and my other daughter Connie went on Facebook, and she found my grandson Michael also on Facebook. They started to communicate with each other, unbeknownst to Michael's parents, my daughter Lori and Sam.

My daughter, Connie made a date to drive to New Jersey to meet Michael, and she took my wife with her. Michael was about 16 years old. He told them he was planning to go into the military service and couldn't wait. He also told them he had two younger brothers, which we had no knowledge of. It was a positive meeting, and my wife, Rachel, thought more meetings could be arranged. That never came to pass.

It was ingrained in Michael that military life was the only worthwhile lifestyle to attain. Time passed, and we learned that Michael had tried to enlist in the Army and had been rejected. He was devastated. His whole life had been geared to military life.

Then we got a call from my cousin telling me to put the news on because there was a story concerning our family. A young man went into a local jewelry store, shot and killed the owner, and then shot and killed himself. We went on the Internet, read the story, and realized it was our grandson Michael. Even though my wife said she would never talk to Lori, she did call their house to offer condolences and our support. My son David also called and left a message that he would offer support in person. He wanted to visit with Lori and her family. She called him back and told him not to bother. No one heard from her again.

What happens when a good and decent person marries a destructive individual like my son-in-law Sam, who destroyed a whole family? This is the question I posed to my wife, Rachel.

I'll tell you what, "Kill Him."

I told Rachel I was willing to sacrifice myself to get rid of him. This feeling was brought on by my frustration at my inability to save our family from this monster. Over time, I became clear-headed and realized I would be sacrificing more than myself. I came to terms with my frustration.

We went for therapy to help us through this terrible time. I told the therapist that I had gone on Facebook to find a friend of Michael's, who might shed some light on the situation. I did hear from one of his friends. He explained that Michael's whole life was geared to being in the military and when he was rejected, for medical reasons, he probably felt his whole life was over, that he no longer had any direction.

The therapist suggested some books about military cults so that we could get an idea of the thinking of these people. She told us that we didn't need to return. There was nothing more she could do to change the circumstances, and we would in time accept the situation.

About two years after my grandson's death, I received a call from my cousin. After chatting with me, she asked to speak to my wife. I went to get her and found that she had died suddenly. There had been nothing physically wrong with her. My daughter Connie went on Facebook and contacted Lori's other son and told him that his grandmother had died and to please tell his mother that "her mother had just died". We never heard one word from her.

THREE

Gambling Equals Family Destruction

I grew up in a very small family. It was just my mom, dad and brother. My parents were married 56 years when my dad passed. My brother Steve lives in Florida with his family, and he is a chiropractor. I graduated from college in New York and decided to move to Florida where my parents had relocated, as I wanted to be near my family. I moved in with them for a while until I could find a job and an apartment.

My horror story begins when I married Paul. We opened a joint bank account, as so many newly married couples do, and deposited our wedding money into the account. When we got back from our honeymoon, I found additional wedding gifts of cash waiting for us. I took them to the bank to deposit them, and the teller informed me we had a total of ten dollars in the account . . . instead of $10,000.00.

Paul had gone to the bank, without my knowledge, and had withdrawn it all. That is when I first found out that he was a compulsive gambler. It turned out that his father was a bookie and a compulsive gambler, and it was all coming out . . . information I never knew about. His brother was also a bookie and a gambler and had spent four years in prison for gambling and dealing drugs on the street, to pay his debts.

I confronted Paul with this and told him I would have the marriage annulled. He promised he would give up gambling, and he prevailed on his father to give us the $10,000.00 to put back into our account. But Paul never really stopped gambling, and he continued throughout our marriage.

When we married, Paul was a shoe salesman. My brother Steve talked him into going back to school to become a Chiropractor, which he did. He went to graduate school in Atlanta, and when he graduated, he opened his own practice. Initially I worked with him. When he started making money, I stayed home, got pregnant and had Barbara. Five years later, I had Richard.

Paul started making a lot of money. The more he made, the more he gambled. When I found out he was gambling again, I confronted him. He agreed to go to Gamblers Anonymous. He only went one time, because he said he could control it, without the program. I stayed in the program Gam-Anon, which supported families of addicts to find out and to understand the addiction.

I decided to get a divorce because it was obvious Paul was not going to stop. I went to see a divorce attorney. He was most unusual in that he insisted I rethink the idea of divorce. He felt I should prepare myself financially to protect the children and myself with some financial security and to wait until the children were older and in school. He thought it would be too hard for me to take care of a seven-month old and a five-year old and go to work. It was a good idea since Paul was paying all the bills, and we wanted for nothing. I changed all the bank accounts to my name and started putting money into those accounts. Paul knew about it, because it was a condition of my staying in the marriage.

At one time, I did speak to my mother-in-law about Paul's gambling. She had raised two sons, who were big gamblers like their father. She told me she had regrets about the lifestyle the children led, but, in fact she enjoyed going to the fancy hotels and living the "high life".

Seven years went by from the time I had consulted the divorce attorney. We lived a very normal life. The kids went to school; we took family vacations with my parents included. All of this stopped one day when the doorbell rang about 4:30 pm. The Sheriff was at the door. He handed me a subpoena. It was from the IRS because Paul owed a quarter of a million dollars in back taxes.

I called my parents first. They said, "You are done." Your kids are older now, and you can have a whole new life ahead of you. I called my husband to find out if he was on his way home. He said he was, and I told him we had to have a serious conversation, and it would be in front of the children. When he arrived, I showed him the subpoena   I told him I was getting a divorce and that he would have to move out immediately.

His excuse was that business was slow and he was using the tax money for us to continue the lifestyle we were used to. But he was gambling all the money away. I did benefit from the lifestyle he was providing, but it was a dishonest one and a loveless one, without any trust.

The children were still young. Richard was only six when I filed for divorce, and Barbara was eleven, and they really did not understand what was happening. My husband never paid the IRS all the money he owed them.

I had a very good divorce attorney. He got me relinquished from all the debt that Paul had incurred, and he made sure that we would have enough money for me to stay at home to take the children to all their activities. I got the house, sole custody of the children, all bank accounts, the maximum amount the state allowed for child support and alimony.

Finally Barbara was off to college, and Richard wanted me to sell the family home and move into a townhouse, so that he could go to a school where his friends were going. I did sell the house, and we did move. Richard was never grateful, or happy, no matter what I did for him. The older he got, the less he loved me, and the fresher he became. He was always very angry, very resentful about the divorce.

My ex-husband remarried Dina, who was in fact, also a gambler. They both said terrible things about me, all of which were untrue. My children had real issues with her and through the years never wanted to visit them.

After we were divorced, Paul got into financial trouble and lost his marital home. He got desperate for money. He had to sell half his practice. He then ended up embezzling money from his partner to pay off his debts. The only way Paul could get away from this trouble was to relinquish his practice and give up his license to practice in Georgia. However, Paul had kept his license to practice in Florida, and they moved to Orlando. They started all over.

My children knew what had happened with his gambling. The children went to visit their father about once or twice a year and came back complaining about his wife and how they hated her. Then he reestablished himself. He started making money again, and gambling again. By this time my children were older and Richard graduated from college. But Richard was becoming a gambler.

When the children reached the age of 18, child support stopped, and I was on my own. I no longer received alimony because I had remarried for a short time and relinquished it. I was doing okay financially because I was working. Then the market crashed, and so did I. I lost my home and everything started falling apart. Paul was making more and more money. I could no longer do anything for my children because I had used up all my money.

Barbara married Harry and they were living in Atlanta. Harry decided to go to chiropractic school and eventually went into practice with Paul. I couldn't believe that Barbara would be dumb enough to want her husband to work with her father after all that had happened. Loving your father is one thing, but trusting him with money is quite another.

Going back to the divorce, there were stock accounts in my name for the children. When the market did well, the accounts did well. When the market crashed, so did the accounts. I never made the money back, and neither did the accounts. They never got replenished. The children accused me of stealing money from their accounts. It was not mismanagement. I had used the money for Barbara's college. She graduated not owing one penny. Richard went through two years of college, not owing one penny. But he was not happy about the remaining years. It is called self-entitlement. They both had new cars, went on all class trips, had expensive clothes. Barbara went to Europe for her high school graduation. I tried to do things that were exciting for both of them.

One day, out of the blue, Paul called and asked to see all the financial statements for all the years, nine to be exact, for the children. I refused and told him it wasn't his business. I could account for all the money that was in the accounts and the expenditures for all those years. The accounts were in my name, and I could have spent the money on myself, but I never did.

I showed my children the accounts and what the money had been spent on. I was not going to take the time to constantly explain that I was responsible, loyal and trustworthy. If they did not trust me because their father was telling them something else, then I was okay with it. I told them that if they didn't trust me after all I had done for them — well then f--- them.

What really started the beginning of the end was when Barbara and Harry got engaged and planned a wedding. She was extremely cold, callous and hateful to me. I didn't have any money to give them toward the wedding, and Paul gave them ten thousand dollars. He became the "good one" because he was giving her the money. She did nothing to show any respect and love for me.

At the wedding, she did not have me walk down the aisle with her. She had me walk down the aisle by myself, and she had her stepmother walk down the aisle, even though for years Barbara had called her every name in the book. They gave her the same honor they gave me. She never called prior to the wedding to say, "Let's get together, let's go over a few things for the wedding". She just said that she and Harry decided to make the wedding the way they wanted it.

She made it very clear to me that my feelings made no difference whatsoever. She totally

ignored me and my family. We were not in any of
the pictures, except one. The Friday night before
the wedding was the rehearsal dinner. It
happened to be my birthday, and I was told there
would be a cake and other stuff to celebrate. There
was nothing.

On the morning of the wedding, Harry's mother
wanted to join Barbara and me in the bridal suite.
I did not feel she belonged there. It was my day
with my daughter. She made a big fuss and got
Harry all upset. I ended up having a fight with
Barbara. I told her how upset I was that my
birthday was totally ignored, and that Harry and
her in-laws were in photos, without me.

The bottom line is that on the morning of the
wedding, I told Barbara that I was done because of
the way I was treated. I said, "I really hope you
get everything you want." But I let it be known
that there isn't a bride married on her wedding
day who thinks her marriage is going to last
forever. "The divorce rate is over 65% and don't
think for one minute that you won't be a statistic
one day," I said. "You are giving up your mother.
I really hope that one day you will get yours". I

felt I was no longer any use to her because I was struggling to get a job, and I had no money.

My daughter had a very close relationship with my mom. My parents spent a lot of time in our home and helped raise them. After seeing the horrible way I was treated by Barbara, my mom had a long talk with her and defended me. That was the last time Barbara spoke to my mom.

Richard was another story. He had a lot of issues because of the divorce, and I think he blamed me. He sided with his sister against me. The way he talked to me was always very insulting. From the time he went to high school, he had absolutely no respect for me as his mother. I really believe he came to hate me. Paul and Dina were feeding him all lies through the years, and he believed them.

I got to a point where I didn't care anymore. I did not want to constantly defend myself. I had to accept that my children had turned on me, the epitome of lack of loyalty — and that was their decision. It is disgusting. Yes, it is all about the money. They gave up their mother, and her whole family, for the MONEY.

FOUR

Religion Changes Family

My parents were divorced when I was seven years old and my sister Carol was five years-old.

In those days it was a shame to be divorced, so we had to keep it a secret. We were not allowed to see my dad. My mother was a very abusive person. She would tell me how fat and ugly I was. She would tell my sister Carol that she had a big head like a basketball. Our biggest fear was that we would be put into an orphanage. My mother would tell us that our father didn't want us, that nobody wanted us. As children this was very frightening. Growing up, this threat was always with us. We had to do everything she asked or demanded of us, and so we did. My childhood was a nightmare, but somehow I managed to survive.

I was introduced to my future husband-to-be, Burt, through a good friend. We dated for about a year before we decided to marry. I told him about my childhood and how abusive my mother had been. We promised each other that we would always show our future children love and respect.

We had three children very close in age: our daughter Selma, and sons Alfred and Sidney. The years went by quickly and were uneventful. The children all went to college. After a few years in college, Sidney informed us that he was not coming back home, but was moving to Maryland, where he bought a condo. We didn't hear from him again. I asked my sister to go to his condo building because they had a doorman. I thought my sister could find out if he was still alive. My sister refused and said "If there is bad news it will find you."

In 1999, my husband suffered a heart attack. I called my three children to let them know their father was to have surgery the next day. Selma and Alfred came to be with us at the hospital. I never heard from Sidney. While waiting at the hospital, Selma, Alfred and I decided that this was our family, and Sidney was no longer a part of it.

After not hearing from Sidney for a few years, I got a call from him telling me he was engaged and wanted to come to the house so we could meet his girlfriend, Lois. If it were up to me, I would have said No, but Burt said Yes, they could come. My husband did not want to make waves. I told Sidney he could come, and I wanted to have a talk with him while he was here.

We sat at the kitchen table, and I asked him what the problem was and why he never came to see his dad in the hospital. He had no answer. I cried. He cried. And I never found out what the problem was. No reason was ever given.

I found out that Lois was involved with Jews for Jesus, and Sidney was becoming more involved with it, and didn't want to tell us. Sidney was planning his wedding, and he asked Alfred to be his best man. Alfred never even responded because he was so angry with Sidney for ignoring the family for so long. We were all invited to the wedding, and although no one wanted to go, I prevailed, which was a big mistake. Sidney did not talk to any of us. My daughter Selma walked out of the wedding crying. None of us could understand why we were invited, and then ignored.

Sometime after the wedding, out of the blue, Burt and I were invited to visit Sidney and Lois. Lois seemed friendly at first. She then started talking to us about Jews for Jesus and gave us pamphlets, which I threw away . . . although I was polite. Sidney had nothing to say to us. My husband thought this was okay because he is also not a talker and that became a bone of contention between us.

Lois was now pregnant, and we were in communication during the pregnancy. We were planning to go to New York, and as it turned out, Lois had just given birth to a little girl, Linda. We went to visit her at home and saw the baby. We stayed a few days and then called to ask if we could see the baby once before we left. We were told they were too busy. That started it. I was fuming. I had just about had it. My husband was just neutral about it. Finally they called and said we could see Linda once more. They were moving, and Sidney was busy working and needed some work to be done around the house. My husband is very handy, so naturally he did what needed to be done.

Lois was pregnant again and was told to stay off her feet. She asked me to please come to help her during this time. Although she had family nearby, they wanted nothing to do with her because they were afraid she would indoctrinate their family into Jews for Jesus. I got right on a plane to visit with them. I stayed a couple of weeks. Lois had an eye problem and had to go to a doctor once a year for special treatments. She asked if I could help out with my granddaughter. I said I would always be glad to help as long as it wasn't tax season, as I worked part time every year.

Lois went to the hospital and unexpectedly gave birth early to a baby boy, Larry. Sidney called and asked me to come and help out. I did go and stayed until she regained her strength. The next time Lois called to have me visit, so she could go for some tests, I said I could not because it was tax season. I suggested an appointment be made right after tax season. She said she could not change her appointment. I said I could not come. She got very upset with us and didn't call for awhile.

I came up with the idea of the whole family going on a cruise together. Lois did not want to go. She said it was not her lifestyle. No TV or newspapers

were allowed in their home, only Jews for Jesus
literature. Sidney persuaded Lois to join everyone
and go on the cruise. It was Linda's birthday. I
bought her an outfit that turned out to be too
small. Lois took it and threw it at me, and said to
take it back. It was obvious she had an attitude
about the cruise.

It was the worst week of my life. We took a suite
all together. Lois was very happy to dump her
children on my other grandchildren—Alfred's
children were teenagers by then. Lois told them
that Linda could have anything she wanted. They
took Linda to the buffet. They got her a hot dog.
Lois took one look at the hot dog and started
screaming that she could not have that because of
the chemicals in it. I said I wanted to take a family
portrait. My daughter offered to watch Lois's kids,
so that they could have a break. Lois told Selma
she couldn't watch her children because "You
don't have any of your own". My daughter was
trying to adopt, so that hurt her.

I then wanted to take Linda to see one of the
musicals, and Lois said, "No. This not our
lifestyle. I don't know why we came. We don't do
these things, and nobody wants anything to do

with us." I then wanted to have lunch with all my grandchildren. And Lois once again said No, but that I could have time with Linda at 2:20 pm by ourselves.

Sidney and I got into a screaming match in front of the kids because he accused all of us of ignoring Lois. We had all offered to be with his kids, but Lois would not allow it. Sidney had no knowledge of Lois's continuous refusal of our efforts to include her and their children. My husband did not take a position. I was very frustrated with Burt. Sidney then said we would never see our grandchildren again. We had one more night together on the cruise. Sidney and his family never came down for dinner. The next day they ran to get off the ship without seeing us and never said goodbye.

My husband and I went to see our therapist because we needed guidance. We totally disagreed about seeing Sidney. The therapist said that in order to see the grandchildren, we would have to look away and ignore what had happened. So back we went to see them. I was not allowed to be alone with the children. When Linda asked me to read to her before going to sleep, Sidney sat outside her room.

I didn't realize at first, that I was never really alone with them. Sidney or Lois was always within hearing distance. We went once or twice more, and I realized that Sidney never spoke to us. I decided I didn't want to go back again. These are people, who are supposed to be religious, but don't "Honor Thy Father and Mother". As much as I want to see my grandchildren, I can't take it anymore.

My husband would go once a year to see the kids and come home and complain. It is about five years since I saw them. My husband has not been there in two years. I have no use for my son. Where are his balls to say to Lois, "They are my parents, and if you don't want to see them, don't go, but I am going to see them?"

In the past, when my grandchildren had birthdays, I would buy bonds in their names. When all this estrangement happened, I realized I had only two grandchildren, Alfred's. I did not want to leave any money to Sidney's children because we no longer had any relationship with them. We went to an attorney and changed our wills, leaving nothing to Sidney and his family.

FIVE

Mind Control

My husband Albert and I met while we were both attending college. We were both raised on farms and found ourselves studying agriculture. We shared a love for the land and never thought about doing anything with our lives except farming. After we graduated, we were married. We moved in with my parents. They had a large farm in Iowa, which was becoming too much for them to handle, and they welcomed our help.

As time passed, we found ourselves building our own house on the property, and we became the proud parents of three children, Marvin, Nate and Olive. They all grew to appreciate the hard work that went into farming, but none showed any interest in following in our footsteps.

The children all graduated high school and went on to college. However, Marvin decided to join the Marines for four years and was sent to Texas for training. One of Marvin's friends had a girlfriend visiting him, who brought her girlfriend Tracey with her. They introduced Tracey to Marvin and according to Marvin, it was love at first sight.

Tracey lived in Missouri and visited with Marvin frequently. Marvin got his orders to go to the south Pacific, and they decided to marry before he left. Tracey went back to Missouri and lived with her parents until Marvin was discharged. Marvin and Tracey decided to put their roots down in Missouri, mainly because Tracey refused to leave her parents. They rented an apartment, and Tracey finished her schooling and became a nurse. Marvin got a job with a large retail business and moved up the ladder in management.

By this time, Tracey and Marvin had three children: Lynn, Debbie and Karl. We were thrilled to have three wonderful grandchildren. Marvin did well financially, and his superiors were pleased with his work. However Marvin was slowly becoming chronically ill with gastro-intestinal problems that no physician seemed able to diagnose. His physical condition worsened, and he was forced to leave his job and go on disability.

During these years, Albert and I visited Marvin and Tracey for a number of holidays and some of the children's birthdays. Marvin and Tracey never visited us because she had to share every holiday with her parents. We never got to be alone with the children. As we got older, it became increasingly difficult for us to make the long drive. We had to stay in a motel, as there was no room for us in their home.

During our visits, we started to notice a pattern emerging between Tracey and Lynn. Tracey was doing everything for Lynn, from buttering her toast to cleaning her room. Lynn was becoming very lazy and spoiled. On one of my visits, I asked Lynn to help me by sweeping the floor. She did not even know how to hold a broom. How scary is that?

This overprotection by Tracey for Lynn caused many problems with Debbie and Karl. They became jealous of all the attention toward Lynn and the lack of it towards them. We tried to discuss this interdependency that Tracey caused, but she refused any discussion. We thought our son Marvin would be more forthcoming, but he too refused. The only good that came from this was it made Debbie and Karl very self-sufficient— a life lesson that served each of them quite well.

Unlike Debbie and Karl, who were doing well in high school, Lynn was barely getting by. Lynn got a part time job and seemed to enjoy it more than school. She also started dating a young man named Matt. They spent time in each other's homes. One day they got into an argument and Marvin overheard Matt being verbally abusive to Lynn. Marvin told Matt he should never talk that way to his daughter and that he was not welcome in the house until he learned to show respect for everyone.

Marvin and Tracey took Debbie and Karl to church one Mother's day and when they returned they found that Lynn had left home, taking all her belongings. Marvin and Tracey went to the store where Lynn worked to confront her, but she wasn't there. It was a week before they finally caught up with her. She was her usual ornery self. She told Marvin and Tracey that she hated living with them and had moved in with Matt and his parents. It was hard to understand why Matt's parents never thought to call the family to tell them Lynn was safe.

As time passed, Lynn made no attempt to contact us. She never returned her parents' calls, or tried

through the initial shock and began planning our approach to the problems of the disease, and we decided we would not tell the children until it was absolutely necessary.

James and Meg had started school, and Dennis was still working as a cabinet maker full time. As the years went by, James became involved in every sport available to him. He was by nature a happy, easy-going child with lots of friends. Meg, on the other hand, was just the opposite. She was moody at times and given to temper tantrums for no reason at all. Meg seemed to be interested in the clothes and things her friends had, and she was never satisfied with what she had.

Dennis started to show some of the symptoms we were forewarned about. He now needed a cane to walk, and I started to drive him to work. It was at this point in time that we finally told the children about Dennis's illness and that we all needed to be supportive of each other. Sometimes my driving Dennis to his various appointments came into conflict with the children's appointments. James seemed to accept this and always managed to get a ride from someone, or he didn't go. He was more accepting of the situation than Meg. James was very compassionate towards his father. Meg was resentful and became sullen.

We all bent over backwards to help her understand what we were all facing. We sought professional help as a family, and individually, for a long time. I thought she would eventually realize she was very much a part of the family unit and would understand that we all depended on each other. After Dennis went from a cane to a walker, he had to stop working, and he went on disability.

I grew up with my dearest friend, Katie. We became friends in first grade and are still great friends. Through the years, the two of us would get great pleasure in creating greeting cards with our original scribble drawings, depicting different professions and hobbies for our friends and families. Eventually, we made rubber stamps of our most popular drawings. It saved us time, and in turn, we used that time to create new scribble drawings. Some of our friends suggested we go into the personal greeting card business. We were both looking to make some extra money and thought it might be just the thing to do. The idea came to fruition and a few months later, we formed our company.

We advertised by going door-to-door to all kinds of businesses and leaving our cards. It started paying off, and then word of mouth propelled us into a growing business. Katie set aside a room in her home, where we could keep all our supplies. This type of business afforded us the luxury of being home with our children while working.

Katie, having been divorced, met her future husband while delivering some of our cards. They became engaged and married shortly thereafter. Katie decided to give up her involvement in the business, as she no longer had the free time. I thought this might be a great opportunity to get Meg involved and thereby spend more time with me. I offered her a weekly salary in the hope that she would feel a sense of accomplishment by being productive. She reluctantly agreed to try. That lasted about one month. Since none of her friends worked, she did not want to be different.

James was off to college with a scholarship. We were thankful, because otherwise he would not have been able to attend college. At this time,

Meg and her friends started looking into sleep-away colleges. Dennis and I discussed community colleges with Meg, explaining we could not afford anything else. She proceeded to have one of her tantrums, accusing us of not caring about her like her friends' parents did. To her, it was always about material things, which she always felt deprived of. We couldn't understand how she could be so callous, considering the struggles her dad endured on a daily basis. We came to the sad conclusion that Meg wanted life to be about her.

Meg did go to a community college, and she decided to study of all things—psychology. She met another student, John, and they married a year later. I felt that Meg was in a hurry to leave our home and that is why she married so quickly. Meg left school to work full time. John finished school and went on to become a teacher. About two years later, Meg gave birth to a baby girl, Amy. We were thrilled and prayed our granddaughter would bring us all closer together. That was not to be.

We called and visited them often. After a while Meg said we were calling too often and that we made her feel as if we were checking up on her. That could not have been further from the truth. We just wanted time with our children. Meg said she would call us and invite us to see Amy, at their convenience. The calls became less frequent. We were very confused about her attitude. I tried calling Meg to discuss the cause of the problem. Most of the time she didn't take my calls.

I finally went to visit her to find out a reason for this odd behavior. She would not even let me into her house. All she would tell me was that she and John were uncomfortable with our visits and would prefer not to see us. Our son James tried intervening by calling them.   Meg would occasionally return his calls and did allow him to visit, but rarely. James did not enjoy the few visits with his sister as she seemed cold and disinterested in him and his life, and after a while he stopped the visits.

While this rejection of us by Meg was going on, I was in contact with John's parents. At first, like us, there didn't seem to be a problem. As time went on, they too were told to wait for an invitation to see Amy. Although their visits became limited, they were allowed to visit once in a while. At my request, they did try to discuss our situation with Meg and John. They basically were told to "mind their own business" if they wanted to continue to see Amy.

We continually tried calling, emailing and writing letters to Meg and John—to no avail. Dennis is now confined to a wheelchair. It is four years since we last saw or heard from Meg and John.

SEVEN

"Buying the House for the Paint"

About thirty years ago, I met Cathy, my future wife. We started dating and eventually we fell in love. We were to be married about one year later. I backed out three times because there was something about her that bothered me. I couldn't quite trust her. We had a very tumultuous relationship. Cathy had a daughter, Sylvia, from a previous marriage. We finally did get married, and I adopted Sylvia, who was a darling little girl. We later had two more children, our son Miles and a daughter, Janice.

We were married for approximately ten years and lived in various apartments and homes in Florida where our children were born and raised. My family lived in the Midwest and Cathy's family lived in Florida.

I was always a salesman and spent all my working years involved in various businesses, one of which was a money management company. I became a vice president and as a corporate officer stupidly allowed them to use my name. When the authorities closed the business down for irregularities, I was left "holding the bag", and I went to jail for a year for a white collar crime I really was not responsible for. None of the others involved served any time.

Cathy was a waitress when she worked. She always believed she could get what she wanted because she was a very attractive blonde. Marrying a pretty woman for her looks is like buying a house for the paint.

For a short time, during my teenage years, I was into the drug scene, but I soon discovered that it was not a path I wanted to continue on. I am now a recovering addict and a member of Narcotics Anonymous. I visit schools and speak about the dangers of drugs in the hope I can guide even one youngster away from drugs.

After many years of a turbulent marriage, I filed for divorce. I was granted full custody of our children, in spite of the fact that our judiciary is tainted against men. For reasons unknown to me,

Cathy never put up any resistance to giving up custody of our children.

When I was granted custody of the children, I was a single father and had great difficulty raising three toddlers. I had to work to feed these children. I didn't have anyone to help take care of them, so I had to hire babysitters.

I was watching television one night, and suddenly there was an advertisement for a Christian organization that invited people who had problems in caring for their children to call for help. I called and told them that I was a recovering addict, and I needed time to adjust to being a single dad, and that I had no family to help with caring for my children. They took children of prison inmates when there were no family members to aid them. It was the first time I was grateful to be an ex-convict. As a recovering addict, I didn't know much about living on life's terms.

After describing my situation, I was told to bring the children to them, and they would help me. I voluntarily left my children there in the hope that I could get my life back on track and be the father they deserved. I went back to Indiana. I called them frequently and visited them. The children were there less than a year when I took them home with me. They had been well taken care of. While we were separated, I was able to secure a good job as a salesman. I also rented a small house in an area where the schools were well rated.

Cathy would contact me from time to time wanting to come back to me. I would take her back because I still loved her. After a while, I realized she only came back whenever she broke up with her then recent boyfriend.

My children did ask about their mom infrequently. I felt they should never be deprived of being in touch with her. Many times I took the children to Florida to visit with her. There were also times when Cathy would break up a relationship with one of her boyfriends and want to come back to us. I always sent her money for a bus ticket. She would stay for a week or two and then leave again.

As part of the program for recovering addicts, we were responsible for "sponsoring" another one to aid in their recovery. I was sponsoring Richard when Cathy came back to us. I found out that Richard was sleeping with Cathy. I told him that she would become pregnant, and he would eventually end up having custody of the child, and Cathy would leave him. That is exactly what happened. At that time, Cathy had given birth to about five children and had custody of none. I told Richard he would have to get another sponsor. I would have nothing more to do with him.

Throughout those years of Cathy's unexpected and impromptu visits, the children reacted to her in varying degrees of anger, resentment and sadness. In their early years, they mostly ignored her. I tried, each time she visited, to explain that she loved them in her own way. She tried to explain that even though she loved them, she couldn't live with them.

As I became more successful in my business and the children were all doing well in school, I decided to start dating. Twice, during my dating years, I thought I had found a woman to share my life. In each case, I thought they had encouraged me to further the relationship. In each case, being the romantic I am, I bought an engagement ring, had a romantic dinner arranged, and in both cases was shockingly turned down. Although each of them claimed they cared for me, neither wanted an involvement with my three children.

The children were teenagers and were all doing well in school. They all graduated from high school. They lived with me while looking for jobs. Eventually they all moved out. My son Miles worked for me for awhile, but I fired him because he was not interested in learning anything. The girls had various jobs. They all lived near me.

This is what I think precipitated the alienation of my children from me. Janice met a young man and decided to get married. I received a call from Cathy telling me she wanted to attend the wedding. Of course, she had no money. I sent her money for the bus trip and paid for her clothing for the wedding. She came for Janice's wedding and never left. Despite the fact that Cathy was never around for our children, except the few times she came to visit through the years, the children astonishingly welcomed her back into their lives.

That was the beginning of an attitude change towards me.

By this time, the girls were both married and had children. I travelled a great deal for my work and when I would return, I would spend time with all my children. As time passed, and Cathy became more ensconced in our children's lives, I was slowly cut out of their lives by shorter and shorter visits, until I was told I was no longer welcome. Sylvia and Janice would not discuss this monumental change in attitude toward me. I tried calling and unexpectedly showing up at their respective homes, in the hope they would give me an explanation for my being so cruelly removed from their lives. The reasons were never forthcoming.

I will not chase disrespectful children because I am not their friend, I am their father. I have since moved on. My hope is that someday when my children have matured, they will hopefully remember and appreciate the struggles and sacrifices I went through to give them a good home as a single parent, while their mother was just a visitor their entire lives.

EIGHT

Choosing Estrangement

I grew up in the San Francisco area with my parents and two younger sisters. We all went to Catholic schools from kindergarten through high school. My father was in the real estate business, and did quite well financially. My mother was a registered nurse, but she only worked part time during our early childhood. Although my parents were quite strict, there always seemed to be an abundance of laughter.

I have fond memories of spontaneous vacations we took at the last minute where we had fun exploring new places. We were a church-going family and every Sunday went to Mass. My family was involved in helping the Christian community raise money for the needy. Looking back, there were no spots of unhappiness. We lived in a much protected environment and grew up being naïve about the world around us.

After I graduated from high school, I went to nursing school. I shared an apartment with another nursing student, Catherine, whom I became very close to. After we became registered nurses, we both got jobs at the same children's hospital. I loved nursing and caring for the children, and I was quite satisfied with the profession I had chosen.

After settling into a routine of working and relaxing, I started to feel a void in my life. I couldn't put my finger on what was bothering me. I felt perhaps I wasn't having any fun, so Catherine and I went to dances, bars, and any social event we were invited to. One day, one of the other nurses I worked with, Patty, invited me to her church, a Protestant one. I really can't explain what happened, but I saw pure joy on the faces of the congregants. I decided to go back a few times, and I realized this church had something I wanted and needed that I hadn't found before. It was not a decision I made lightly, but after much consideration I gave up Catholicism and became a Protestant. It was the biggest upheaval in my family's history. My family actually disowned me.

I met my husband-to-be, Simon, at a "career age activity" through the Protestant church. He was, at the time, still in the army. He had joined for four years in order to get a free education. After being discharged, he chose to go to an airline school. By this time we were married and had moved in with Simon's parents until Simon finished school. My parents still wanted nothing to do with me and did not attend our wedding. Simon finished his airline training and through the school got a job in Detroit with a major airline. We moved to Detroit and lived there for eleven years.

I worked full time as a nurse, and Simon started his career cleaning airplanes and over the years rose to being a supervisor of daily activities with different service agents. Because of his work with the airlines, we were entitled to fly free anywhere in the world.

About two years later, our son Hank was born. It was at this time that my parents finally reunited with me. It was a very happy reunion. Simon and I decided we wanted another child and after a few years of trying, we started going for medical testing. We were told that I could not have any more children. It was a difficult time for us, but Simon and I agreed to try adoption. We tried to adopt an American baby for eight years, without success.

One Sunday we went to a church picnic in a very large park. There was another church group also having a picnic. I noticed one of the families had a Korean baby with them. Simon and I approached them and found out about an adoption agency in Oregon that worked with one in South Korea, bringing Korean babies into America. We got in touch with the agency and proceeded to take the necessary steps towards adopting a Korean baby. While waiting for the baby, our son, Hank told us he only wanted a baby brother to play ball with, not a baby sister. It took two years until we got Lisa into our arms, and when Hank saw her, he said he changed his mind and would take care of his baby sister.

We met other parents, through the adoption agency, all having adopted Asian babies. We formed a group and met once a month for at least two years. It worked quite well for everyone. Then, Simon was transferred to Florida. Hank was nine and Lisa was two. We were happy with the move, mainly because of the weather, which made life easier for us.

My parents continued family visits on a regular basis as did Simon's parents. Everyone made a big fuss over the children, and everyone treated Lisa like a little princess. The agency we adopted Lisa from started a summer camp for Asian children. It was unique because it taught the language, culture, food, dress, music and art of the different Asian countries. Lisa went for two weeks every summer and lived within the Korean culture. She went to the camp for seven years and loved every minute of it.

When Lisa was in junior high school, she started questioning us about her birth parents. We had very little information about her background to share with her, but we offered her trips to South Korea a number of times. Although we tried talking to her about this subject from time to time, she made it clear that she did not want to go to Korea. She felt that her birth parents had abandoned her. She seemed content living with us.

At about the time Lisa started high school, she started rebelling by staying out late, smoking, and using foul language. Overnight she turned into a "teenage terror" and from what we learned, it was part of growing up.

Simon and I had a college fund for each of the children. We gave Hank his money when he went to college. Lisa decided she did not want to go to college, but she wanted to take a course in creative movie making in London. She wanted her money in one lump sum. We were not happy about giving her all of the money, but we had very little choice since we had given Hank all of his funds. She went to London and took the six month course and found it to be a waste of time, but she managed to use up all the money.

Lisa decided not to come home, but to stay in London with friends. They all decided to join a youth organization, which basically was a missionary group, looking for monetary help for the underprivileged while "spreading the word of God". Lisa was sending letters to family and friends asking for money. At this time, she was not working and was actually using the money collected, for herself. She eventually agreed to come home. Lisa was a different person than the one that had left for London. She was using terrible language, experimenting with drugs, and totally disrespectful. She was not living up to the Christian values expected of her. She was still soliciting for funds under the guise of the missionary group, but still using the money for herself. Lisa was in fact a "fraud". In spite of this, we offered to get her professional guidance, to support her until she got a job, to live with us, but none of this was acceptable. So we had to show "tough love", and we threw her out of our home.

Since Lisa could still use the free airline passes, she decided to go to Poland. She spent five years there, painting houses, painting wall murals and anything she could do to support herself. She travelled throughout Europe, and not once did she come home to see us.

In her travels, she met an old friend and together they went to South Korea. Lisa decided to stay in order to search for her birth mother, and her friend decided to come back home. After checking out a number of possibilities, Lisa finally made contact with her birth mother. I think that Lisa had a vision of being back with her mom and her mom's family, and that they would accept her into their world, and finally life would be sweet. That was not to be. Her mother could not publically acknowledge her as Lisa was an illegitimate child. In Korean society the family would be shunned. Therefore, her mother could only see her secretly.

While all this was going on, our son had married and has three children. I was diagnosed with MS, and Simon and I divorced. The rare times we heard from Lisa, we all begged her to return to America. She finally told me she had decided to remain in South Korea. It is ten years since any of us have seen her.

True estrangement—Lisa could see me if she chose to, but she doesn't choose to.

NINE

Discarded Family

I was raised in a loving home with a brother, who I am still very close to. We have a large family of aunts, uncles and cousins. We were always having them visit us, or we would go to their homes. My parents played cards every Saturday night with their friends, who then became part of our extended family. I grew up with three very close girlfriends and feel lucky that we are still close with each other.

I had a close friend Frank, not a boyfriend. We spent good times together for a number of years. He was drafted into the Army at the end of World War II, along with a friend of his, Ryan. Frank carried my photo with him, and Ryan asked if he could write to me. Frank asked me if it would be okay. I said, I didn't mind. Ryan and I corresponded with each other. Then, one night my doorbell rang, and when I went to answer it, Ryan was standing there asking to see my sister. I said, "I am my sister". We unexpectedly both felt an immediate connection. We started dating, and a year later we were married.

We moved into a three-story walk-up apartment. Ryan went back to school to study engineering, and I went to work. After Ryan graduated, we moved to Ohio because the jobs were more plentiful there for engineers. He found a good job, and we eventually bought a lovely house and raised our two children there, our daughter, Helen and our son, Charles. When we first moved to Ohio we had no friends or family. One of Ryan's business associates had a party and invited everyone he knew, who were from other parts of the country. The couples we met became our lifelong friends. We hosted and cooked and made all the holiday dinners for our friends because we had a ping pong table that accommodated everyone. Our friends became our family.

Looking back at those times, I would have to say it was the best of times. We had a happy loving home, surrounded by a wonderful group of friends. We had a pretty good life. There is nothing I could point to that would prepare me for the eventual loss of our daughter, Helen. When our children were in school full time, I decided to go back to school. I became a computer programmer, and a systems analyst.

After our son, Charles graduated from college as a journalist, he decided to move to California, and he became involved with Caesar Chavez because he is a socialist like his grandmother and mother. Helen had wanted to study architecture and mechanical drawing, but the school would not permit it because she was female. My husband went to the school and fought with them, and they finally allowed her to study mechanical drawing. Our daughter Helen met a young man Kirk at school. She brought him home to meet us. Kirk seemed like a nice young man, studying to become a teacher.

Although Kirk was of a different religion, we had no objection to their marrying since they seemed to care about each other. Kirk's parents felt the same way as we did. The children eventually married. We made them a small wedding in our backyard because my husband was having medical issues. Shortly after they were married, they moved to another city because Kirk got a teaching job.

In the meantime, Ryan took a job in Maine, and we leased our home. He worked there for awhile, and then we moved back home. He then took a job in Illinois, and we sold our home. We saw Helen and Kirk and were always in touch with Charles. We then moved to Colorado where Ryan got a job, and we thankfully stayed there about twelve years.

My daughter Helen had a baby boy, Stuart, and we visited with them for a few days. Everything seemed to be okay. It was always okay as long as my husband was living. About two years later she had her second baby, a little girl, Wendy. We had not seen Helen and her family since the birth of Stuart because her husband, Kirk was afraid to fly, and he would therefore not permit any of them to fly because he thought they might die. We did visit them and saw the new baby Wendy, along with Stuart, for a short visit as my husband Ryan had had a stroke, and it was not easy for him to travel.

My son Charles left California and moved to Maine where he met and married Rhonda. We went to the wedding. My daughter Helen did not attend as she was pregnant. It was a big wedding.

I was upset that Helen refused to go to the wedding. Charles just accepted it because he was not close to Helen anymore, as she had chosen to remove herself from all of us. On our way back to Colorado, my husband got sick again and died shortly thereafter. Charles and Rhonda and Helen came to Ryan's funeral. Helen's husband did not attend. Charles and Helen had very little to say to each other, and really they never had. They didn't have words, but they were never close, and as time went on, they drifted further apart.

I decided to move back east. There was very little for me in Colorado. I chose Massachusetts since Charles was in Maine, and that was not too far for us to see each other. Helen and her family visited me just once in the years I lived there. I saw my brother all through the years. Thankfully, we remained quite close. Charles and Rhonda had two children, Adam and Paula. They moved back to Massachusetts after I moved to Florida. They subsequently divorced, and Rhonda moved back to Maine. They had a friendly divorce, and they still see each other and spend time together with their children.

After I moved to Florida, my daughter Helen visited me only once with her two daughters, because my son-in-law would not fly and would not let my grandson fly. The only way I could see them would be to go to Ohio. The visits to them were far from pleasant as Kirk was verbally abusive to Helen, and he was very unfriendly to me. I made my visits short. I tried talking to Helen about Kirk's behavior, but she would not listen to anything derogatory about him. I couldn't discuss this with my grandchildren until they were older. They were all aware of the abuse. My granddaughter Wendy told me she had wanted her mother to leave her father, but Helen would not listen.

My son Charles made a birthday party for me in Florida and insisted that Helen attend. She came alone and stayed two days. I didn't see her again until my granddaughter Wendy's wedding and again at my younger granddaughter Evelyn's wedding. At that time, I asked my daughter why she never called me considering I was growing older and could be in poor health. I told her I felt neglected. All she could say was a quick, "I am sorry". Not even, I AM S-O-O SORRY. She never did call.

The best way to describe her behavior is to say she basically divorced her whole family, for reasons only known to her. There was never an argument or an incident I could point to as the cause of her behavior. My brother has children and grand-children, and she has not met some of them and has no communication with any of them. Helen and her family have not gone to one family function in all the years she's been married. He won't go, and he will not allow her to attend.

The only one I am in constant contact with is my granddaughter, Wendy. She calls me all the time and visits with me. She is expecting a baby, and I will become a great grandmother.

I went to see my attorney, and I cut Helen and two of her children out of my will. I am leaving my estate to my son, his two children, and my granddaughter Wendy.

I am sad that I don't have a daughter anymore. I am trying to move on with my life, and I am grateful that I have a caring son and grandchildren that love me.

TEN

The "No" List

My name Is Phyllis and my husband's name is Marty. We have been married many years. We have two sons, Oscar who is in a mental hospital, and Norm, who we have been estranged from for about four years.

Norm had always been the 'good son', always excelled in school and sports, and always loving and concerned about his parents. He attended an Ivy League college and received an MBA degree. He was a happy-go-lucky man. He lived in the city, and we saw him often — at least once a week. He would visit with us and spend a Sunday with his Dad just watching football, or we would go into the city for brunch with Norm.

Through his college he was hired by an international corporation, and he became a Vice President for that company. He stayed with the company for ten years. He had a job that he loved, and he had lots of friends.

He met a girl, Rose, on vacation and became enamored with her. She was very well educated, seemed to be in love with Norm, and was very warm towards Marty and me. She told her mother that she was not dating anyone else. Rose gave Norm a very expensive present on their six-month anniversary, and Norm gave one to her. Rose then told Norm she wanted an engagement ring. He asked us to start looking for a special ring for her. Even though we did not share the cost of the ring, Norm was anxious for our approval.

They were married and had a magnificent wedding. We were very happy and thought we had the beginning of a healthy relationship with Rose. They went to Australia on their honeymoon, and when they returned we noticed a slight change in Rose's attitude toward us. Norm did not call as often as he used to, and he didn't want to talk to me. He only wanted to talk to Marty. I put up with that for a while. I thought maybe he didn't know how to be a son and a husband at the same time.

We realized that we were not spending much time with them, and when we did it was always with Rose's family too. Never with just us. After a while, it became obvious that we were really not part of the family.

Norm continued his employment, but seemed less and less happy with it. He was making a substantial amount of money and taking many company trips. He was making some decisions about movement in the company, which we did not agree with. Subsequently, his decisions led to a change in his position — to a lesser one. He was not a happy man. He let the powers that be know his feelings because he was convinced he was secure in his position within the company.

He was laid off and had to find employment elsewhere. Norm started taking lower position jobs instead of looking for a job on the level he was used to. He went from one job to another and never was able to get a "career position" again. Norm has a character flaw. He will never get a really good job because his karma is screwed up. He messed with his self-esteem and doesn't feel good about himself.

As his career was in a downward spiral, Rose's position was getting stronger. He couldn't afford an apartment on his own income. They could only do so because of Rose's job. Rose was getting stronger as Norm was getting weaker. Rose loved her job and felt fulfilled. She had never planned on working like this.

They appear to be a loving couple, but I don't believe it. Rose, for some reason, is dependent on her parents, and so they spend all their free time with them. She makes all the social arrangements. Why doesn't Norm say, "My parents live only an hour away—I want to see them, with or without you"? Why? Because Norm is weak of character. He has had to conform to another personality in order to make his life calm. He knows she is explosive.

Rose became pregnant about a year after they were married. I felt that Norm was not looking forward to parenthood. I think he was afraid that he might have a child, who would be emotionally disturbed like his brother Oscar. She told Norm it would not change his life. She had an easy pregnancy and gave birth to a beautiful baby boy, Jimmy. We went to the hospital and spent quality time with them. We assured Norm that the baby was normal.

As time went by we got to see the baby often. When they came to our house I noticed that Rose seemed anxious, and then they started arriving later and later, thereby cutting their visits shorter. When we would visit them, we would find that Rose's parents were always there. We were never alone with the children. I did become unnerved by that.

Since we spent much less time with Jimmy than her parents, we felt we should have time alone with the baby, but that was not to be. While Rose was still home with Jimmy, we would bring dinners to them, and I would take her to lunch. I don't know if I was doing the right thing. I got the feeling she wasn't interested. As time went on, she invited us to classes with the baby. We hoped our relationship was developing.

My son then arranged to have lunch with Marty. At that lunch Norm told Marty that his wife really did not like me. This took him completely by surprise. He said he couldn't understand that, since his mother had been so generous to Rose. Norm never really explained the reasons. I felt Marty made a mistake in not insisting, at that time, that we all get together to find a solution to the problem. That never did happen.

We purchased a home in Florida and became "Snow Birds", spending half our time up North and half down South.

The last time Norm was in Florida, we were all together by the pool. Norm sat in a corner isolated from his wife, child and us. I think he had to change in order to keep sanity in his life. I think he is living in an abusive relationship — not physically, but verbally and emotionally. From the time they arrived, it was a very difficult visit. When my husband went to hug Norm, it was like hugging a tree. We took them out for dinner that night to a place that was "child" friendly, and we thought it was a lovely family outing. The next day was a nightmare. I can only say "all hell broke loose". Rose didn't like the food served, even though she had sent us a list of what to buy.

We told Rose to consider the visit a vacation for them and that we would be happy to help out with the baby. We fed and diapered Jimmy and got up in the middle of the night to take care of him. There was an incident at breakfast. We fed him before Rose and Norm woke up. It turned out that was the wrong thing to do because it wasn't his breakfast time. Norm came in screaming telling me I shouldn't have done that in spite of the fact the baby was hungry. It became a week of screaming.

It culminated in Rose insisting on leaving immediately. It was only 7:00 am, and Marty was still sleeping. They woke him up from a sound sleep and told him they wanted to leave, and he responded that he thought it was a good idea. That was probably the worst sentence he could have uttered. Marty took them to the airport. Much to our dismay, they ended up sitting in the airport many hours. When we found out about the delay, I called and said we would stay at the airport and help with the baby, or come and pick them up and take them back to the house and they could leave the following day. They refused all offers. They wanted no part of us. They went home.

Earlier I had made a 65th birthday party for my husband, Marty. Norm made a wonderful speech about the two of them. Now five years later, he doesn't even send a card for Marty's 70th birthday.

I sometimes think about the possibility of one of us dying and wonder if Norm would be able to express any emotion, or if he just wouldn't care.

About a week after they left, we received a list of rules and regulations. We had to humbly apologize, and they had to feel that we were utterly sincere. I had no idea what I was apologizing for. We subsequently received a phone call telling my husband that we were no longer a part of their family. He said his family consisted of Rose, Jimmy and Norm. My husband sat down and cried like a baby, and that resulted in absolutely no communication between us for two years.

I had made several phone calls during that time to Norm, telling him we missed him terribly and loved him and his family. He did not respond until he must have realized that Jimmy missed us. He allowed us to spend about two hours during the day with Jimmy and his nanny. We were not allowed to share Jimmy's birthday parties. We never wavered and did not miss a chance to spend those days with him. We sent cards and gifts and made phone calls, but never got any response.

After some time, I decided the only way to try to improve the situation, was to be extremely kind to Rose and to put our son in the background. It seemed to help. We got to see them on occasional holidays and to go to Jimmy's birthdays.

Rose became pregnant with their second child. We were not told about it. After their second son, Larry was born, we realized we had a different relationship with this baby. We were not included in anything going on, and we did not have the closeness we had with Jimmy. We were never allowed to take Larry to the park for a walk.

In reference to the question, is it painful or too torturous to see the children rarely, with all the rules and regulations, or is it better to just pack it in and go on with our lives? I discussed this with Marty. He said he would never give up the opportunity to see the children no matter how infrequently, because it was an extension of our family. It brings joy to his life. If I were alone, I think I might be able to do it. The two hours we get to see them is pure pleasure. The children do get to see us and yes, it is very painful. I guess the answer is Yes, it is worthwhile because when I get older I will have these memories.

I had an opportunity, little as it was, to share time with them. I did my best to provide love, pictures and books. I mail them things. I tell them they are lucky to have a second set of grandparents. I do as much as I am allowed to bring happiness to the children. I hope they will remember us. We have our New York home up for sale and eventually we will be in Florida full time. I am sure this will make it difficult to see them.

Norm found a way to shrink his personality. His old self is gone and cannot be brought back. I call him a "POD" person (person on drugs). He looks similar except much thinner since becoming a vegan.

The following is the 'NO LIST' that my son had us follow:

Do not ask anything about their apartment rental situation.

Do not ask about Norm's job. (We could discuss Rose's.)

Do not ask about buying or leasing a car.

Do not sing to the baby.

Do not use Yiddish words when speaking to the baby.

Do not question anything about the baby or give any input of any kind.

Do not buy the baby clothes, only toys.

Do not visit on weekends. (They are only for her immediate family.)

Do not give the baby any treats when out with him.

I blame my son for not caring enough to fix a situation he could have — had he chosen to do so.

ELEVEN

A Lesson Not Learned

My name is George, and I am now a happily divorced man. My story begins many years ago. My wife Betty and I had been married a few years when we decided to have a baby. Deciding to have a baby and actually having one are two vastly different things, we found out. After months of trying, we sought medical help. After a period of time of testing and trying fertility drugs, we were told we were not candidates for those procedures and should consider adoption.

We applied to various adoption agencies, and after five years, we were finally approved and our daughter Doris came into our lives. It was one of the most joyous times for us. Doris was a delightful baby and an easy child to raise. When Doris started school, Betty and I applied for a second adoption. Soon after the application was filed, much to our amazement, Betty became pregnant. She lost that pregnancy, and it became a difficult time for us. However, she became pregnant again, and we became parents of our son

Mitchell. We doted on him and treated him like a little prince, but he was a difficult child right from the beginning.

As Mitchell grew, he attended various public and private schools. He attended a school where two grades were put together and the children could decide what they wanted to do in class. Mitchell did not do well in that school. Betty and I thought he needed more structured teaching. As he grew, we decided to send him to a prep school, where he showed improvement. During all this time, our daughter Doris was going to public schools. She made lots of friends and enjoyed her classes. Her formative years were unremarkable.

Mitchell went off to college. He became a star athlete and a thief. He was arrested for stealing money from the lockers of the players. He was arrested for stealing money from envelopes for the aides in school around Christmas time. He went to college to become a basketball star, but we sent him to college to become smarter. He was thrown out of a number of colleges before he went to one to study to become a chef. He brought home his first report card with all "D's" and one "C". I told him I preferred "A's" and "B's". But I was realistic, and I said if he didn't get at least "C's", I would not pay for his schooling. The next report card he did get all "C's". However, he was lazy and did only the minimum to get by. Lying and stealing was his way of life.

He graduated from college and was working in a restaurant in mid-Manhattan. He complained to us that he had no evenings or weekends off. We told him to stop complaining as he was getting good experience. We reminded him that he was in a service business that required his attendance evenings and weekends. Mitchell was unhappy and decided to quit his job. He went from job to job until he was hired by a hotel chain in their food service department.

Before this, while still in New York, Mitchell met a girl about eleven years older than he. Betty was not happy about it. I could care less. Mitchell finally got married and moved with Shirley to Florida. We then moved to Florida permanently. We decided to invite Mitchell and Shirley for brunch one Sunday. We ended up waiting and waiting. Brunch to us is between 11:00 and 12:30. I finally called Mitchell to see if he was alright, and I realized that I had awakened him. We were quite upset and told him not to bother coming to the house. He argued with me and said that I had an attitude. It was downhill from there.

While all of this was happening with Mitchell, Betty informed me that she wanted a divorce. We had a terrible fight, and she called the police. They took me away in handcuffs because she told them I had abused her, which I had not. The police did not believe me. (It certainly is a woman's world out there.) I went to jail overnight. At the hearing the next morning, I was served with divorce papers. The charges were dropped against me.

I was married forty-six years when we finally divorced. I waited that long because of the children. I wanted them to be grown and on their own. When we divorced, my wife cut me out of her medical plan. My son Mitchell and his wife, having the same initials as my wife and I, were getting prescriptions for drugs under my name. I finally found out about it because I was being billed by doctors I'd never heard of. It was a criminal act that Mitchell was doing. I called the shop where he and his wife worked. She answered, and I left a message for him to call me. I subsequently got a letter, all in red ink, threatening me, and telling me I should never contact them again.

I called the Florida State Insurance Department and turned them in for obtaining drugs under a false name. It was the second time they had done this to get drugs. Mitchell was taken to jail, but released. Later he was arrested again for the same offense. This time he was made to pay the money back to the insurance company. He never went to jail for this offense. I am truly sorry he didn't go to jail. It might have taught him a good lesson.

I am a survivor, and no one is going to take me down—not even my own son.

Doris is happily married. Her husband is very good to her. I have a wonderful relationship with her and my son-in-law's family. We spend good quality time together.

TWELVE

"Cult of One"

My husband and I have been married 40 years and have two children, Todd is 37 and Sally is 33. My son Todd is married and has two children and lives near us. My daughter Sally is married and has two children and does not live near us.

Growing up, Sally was always a happy loving child. At age 15, Sally met a local boy named Max, who we had heard had mental problems. We tried to discourage her from seeing Max. We didn't know what the diagnosis was, but he constantly got involved in altercations with teachers and people in authority. We knew he would be a bad influence on her. Sally wasn't dating him, so we didn't put any pressure on her not to see him. When she became a high school senior, she did start to date him.

But then she went off to college, and he went to another college. He seemed to need a "safety person" around him, so he found another girl and became the center of her attention. He stayed with this other girl for two years, but all this time he was still calling my daughter. He constantly complained to Sally about his girlfriend, and this got our daughter so upset, she became bulimic. When she came home from school for vacation we arranged for therapy sessions. She seemed to be doing better and met someone else. She switched colleges to start anew. However, every time she came home on school breaks, Max called Sally and showed up at our house.

This basically continued throughout her college years. She finally graduated and was going on to graduate school to become a social worker, and a therapist (which I think is ironic).When she came home from college she started seeing Max again, much to my dismay, and she broke off her relationship with the other young man.

When we first met Max, he was unable to look me in the eye when speaking to me. He seemed out of it, especially when he took my daughter to the prom. Some of the reasons we didn't like him were because he did not come into the house, and the few times he did, he did not talk to us. He only wanted to possess Sally. We lived in the same area as Max's parents and met them only a few times.

They were divorced. His father was a Viet Nam vet. Max lived in a big house with his mother.

Sally told me that Max was in a bad way mentally, and she wanted me to talk to Max to see if I could help him. I did see him and decided to call his mother to suggest he get professional help. She seemed appreciative of the call, but I don't know if he ever did get professional help.

Max would not come to our house, and Sally would spend her time at Max's He wouldn't call on the house phone. We told Sally we didn't want her seeing Max because he was not a stable person. We told Sally that he wanted to possess her and she would end up without friends or family. We tried to explain that someone who is so needy isn't necessarily in love, and that Sally could end up being in 'A CULT OF ONE'.

Max's mother passed away. His mother had been his lifeline. Sally became his surrogate mother and moved into his house part time. She would come home with her dirty clothes and throw them on the floor. She then started smoking pot. I could smell it throughout the house. She was going to graduate from school at the time. Max dropped out of college after two years. He was working as a delivery boy for a restaurant.

My son, Todd and Sally had always gotten along very well. So when Todd and his girlfriend came for a visit, they naturally wanted to go out with Sally and her friends. Sally said she was too busy. We suggested that Todd drive by Max's house to see if Sally was there. She was not. The next day we got a call from Sally. She said someone had broken into her car window. Sally told us that Max blamed Todd for this. We told Sally that was ridiculous. Her brother would have absolutely no reason to do that. We told her the insurance would pay for the repairs. She was okay with that.

All of a sudden I heard screaming outside, and the noise was getting closer to our home. I looked out my window and saw Max coming to our house. He rang the doorbell, and continued screaming that Todd broke her car window. I did not let him in. Sally was next door and heard the screaming. She stood next to him while he screamed at me, and she did nothing. I told Max he could never come into our house, and I told Sally if she continued seeing Max, she could not live in our house anymore.

I subsequently had an errand to do and left the house for an hour. Upon my return, Max was waiting for me with flowers. He apologized to me. I should have thrown the flowers away, but because I'm a kind person I invited him in. I tried explaining how we were a family, and we wanted Max and Sally to share time with us. I tried to explain to Sally that a person could be ill, but also very devious. After the car incident, Sally had nothing to do with her brother.

Sally was still staying with Max and his dad at their house. Before Max came into Sally's life, Sally was into looking her best and wearing lovely clothes. The more involved she became with Max, the more she looked like a bag lady. I decided to talk to Max's father. I didn't want Sally sleeping at their house because she was going to graduate school, and that meant she had to be driven to the train station and picked up at night.

As it turned out, while I was telling Max's father that they were smoking pot and that there were a number of problems with Max and his behavior, Max and Sally showed up. Max went crazy and attacked my husband by grabbing his neck. His father had to pull Max off. I said to Sally, "Did you see what Max did to your father?"

She replied, "He deserved it." We went home and I gathered all of Sally's clothes and went back to Max's and threw all her clothes and belongings on their lawn and driveway. A few days after that, Max's father made them move out.

They got an apartment. Max was working, Sally was going to graduate school, and she got a job as a waitress to pay for her school. We saw Sally occasionally at the restaurant where she worked, but never with Max. She was friendly and asked if we could help pay for graduate school. We paid half because we had made that agreement with her before she started graduate school.

She called one day to announce that she was getting married and she asked us to plan and make the wedding for her. We believed every girl should have her "Day in the Sun". We spared no expense. At the wedding Todd asked the band to play music to dance the "Hora", a Jewish folk song, because their grandparents would enjoy it. Sally made a terrible scene, screaming at Todd that he had no right to do that, and she never wanted to talk to him again. Sally and Todd never spoke to each other again. That was the end of a close brother and sister relationship. There were many incidents that Max created to divide and conquer Sally's family relationships.

After the wedding mess, Sally called us occasionally. We felt like we had lost our daughter. We began drinking heavily and taking all kinds of pills. We began seeing a therapist because we could not accept the loss of our daughter. It was a very dysfunctional time for us, so we decided to sell the house and move to Florida. We did get to speak to Sally to tell her we were moving. Surprisingly, she seemed happy that we were moving. In fact, she visited us several times by herself. She had graduated and got a job as a social worker.

She called to tell us she was pregnant and losing the baby. We flew up to be with her, and we stayed with cousins in their house. A few months later, Sally was pregnant again—a "high risk pregnancy". She had a baby girl three weeks early, so we flew back to New York. We went to Sally's house and found it disgustingly filthy. We both cleaned the bathrooms until they were usable, and we bought the baby furniture. We were there every day to help them.

We were then invited for Thanksgiving. They were decorating for Christmas. I asked if they would also have a Menorah, and Sally said, "No", she no longer believed in Judaism. She became a Methodist. The house was very cold, and we asked if they could raise the temperature. They said, "No", so we slept with our clothes on. We even offered to pay for heating the house. Max yelled at me, "I find you offensive, and if you cannot shut up, you have to get out of this house. All the time Max was shouting at us, Sally never said one word. Max took away her name, her religion and her persona.

Sally had to go back to work when the baby was three months-old, and the baby was to go to day care. We offered to stay for a month so the baby would not go to day care right away. She agreed to let us baby sit. However, when Sally went to work we found all the doors to all the rooms were locked. If we needed something for the baby, we could not get into the room. I called Max to find out why everything was locked, and he became abusive. We left the next day.

Sally and I emailed occasionally — you might say about generic topics — weather, etc. for a long time. I decided to write her a letter. I hoped we could work things out. Sally told me we didn't exist anymore. I found out she was eight months pregnant and a high risk pregnancy again. She never told us about the birth of their son. We started sending gifts for the children. They were never acknowledged, neither did we ever get photos of the children. We finally did get a letter calling us "paranoid," "untrustworthy", and saying, "To hell with you." She became mean, cruel and abusive to me. I don't think she is my daughter anymore. My daughter died years ago, and I feel somehow relieved. It had evolved into a complete "CULT OF ONE".

THIRTEEN

Different Therapist?

I grew up in a family with two sisters. Our parents were loving but strict with us. We were taught family values and were expected to follow all the rules and regulations, and not bring any shame to our family. We lived in a small community where everyone knew everyone else. I didn't get along with my middle sister. I came home from college one weekend, and I was told to pick up my sister. We got into an argument, and I called her a "bitch". When we got home she told my father, and he pulled me by my hair into the bathroom and washed my mouth out with soap. I was twenty at the time. My dad strongly believed in respect for all. We were practicing Roman Catholics and went to church every Sunday and were expected to be observant.

I graduated from college with a nursing degree and promptly got a job in a nearby hospital. While working there I met my husband to be, Edward. We were married about one and a half years, when Edward had a massive heart attack and died. At the time, I was three months pregnant with our daughter, Emily.

About three years later, I met Martin, and we were married and had two children together, a son Phillip, and a daughter Diane. I think the problems with Emily began when I had my other two children. Emily was about four years-old. Up until the time Phillip and Diane were born, Emily had been spoiled by everyone, first because she had no father, and then she was Edward's only child, and his family treated her like a true princess.

The children were five, eight and eleven when we moved to Florida. Martin retired and thought the move would be good for all of us. We were trying to work out our marital problems: the biggest problem being his verbal abuse to me and his slapping the children around when I was not home. I would not tolerate abusive behavior, so I divorced Martin. I took a job as a health care nurse and sometimes worked fifteen hours a day, seven days a week, in order for us to survive. I did manage to take the children to their piano lessons, soccer games and whatever appointments were necessary. Was I the best Mom? The constraints of my job prevented me from that. I was the best I could be.

My ex-husband started telling the children what a terrible mother I was and causing friction among all of them. Emily was into her teens and becoming rebellious. She did see a therapist. It did not seem to help. She argued with me about everything and told me how much she hated me and that she wished I was dead. Since I had not grown up in that type of atmosphere, I found it difficult to handle. I would punish her by taking privileges away from her. I then started reading her diaries. She was thirteen years-old and I was shocked to read that she was planning to have sex with someone. I knew I had to help her because she was a very self-centered egotistical child. She was a control freak, who always had to have her own way. I decided to send her to a private school, not a fancy school, but one that could handle children with problems. It was like a farm.

Emily was at 'the farm' about five months when her grandparents and aunt sued me for custody of her person and her property. The court case took two years to complete. The family wanted to have me and Emily tested for psychological problems.

In the findings of the court, I was found to be competent. The only suggestion the court made was to take Emily out of the private school, and place her in a public school.

I continued to have problems with Emily not obeying the rules. She was allowed to see her grandparents by court order. Finally, one day Emily told me she wanted to move in with her aunt and uncle, the relatives who took us to court. I told Emily she could move out whenever she wanted to. This was a shock to her. She thought I would put up a fight, but I called her bluff. She came back a few days later and informed me she would move.

The relatives she moved in with lived a few blocks from us. So after school as she was walking to their house, she would pass me, as I was getting the mail, and we would say hello to each other. It became apparent that she wanted to start a new life. However, my sister-in-law, Mary, my ex-husband's sister, went to court to sue me again, this time for child support. I agreed to give her $300.00 per month for as long as Emily lived with them.

About a little over a year later, Mary called begging me to take Emily back. She complained bitterly that Emily would not listen and would not obey any home rules, and she didn't have time to spend with her own children. She also found that Emily was climbing out of her bedroom window every night. I reminded her that she had wanted Emily to move in with them.

I told her I would take her back under one condition — she could not tell Emily she couldn't live there anymore. She would have to make it as miserable as she could until it became Emily's idea to move out. It worked. Emily came home, and for about one month she behaved. After that she started giving me more grief. Her grades in school were falling, and her attitude was quite negative.

My father had moved in with me after my mom died. It was a good situation for both of us. My dad was a golfer and invited some people to come to Florida and play golf with him. One of the men brought his nephew Jack with him. We found ourselves enjoying each other's company. I subsequently married Jack. We continued to have problems with Emily and found that at age fifteen she was sexually active. The only thing I could do was to make sure she had protected sex.

Then it was time for Emily to go to college. For the first few years she lived at home and commuted to school because she didn't want to leave her boyfriend. However, her boyfriend didn't have any money, and he kept borrowing from Emily. When Emily decided to go away to school, she insisted I give her all her money, so she would not have to ask me for anything. I agreed, but warned her that this money would have to last throughout school.

She eventually broke up with her boyfriend because he was not earning any money. She did graduate from school as a speech pathologist. She and her girlfriend decided to move to California where she got a job. About one year later, there was a major earthquake that destroyed everything around her.

A new friend talked her into moving to Atlanta, which is where he was from. He introduced her to lots of young people. Emily got a job, settled into her new environment, and met Kenneth, her husband-to-be. His family was wealthy and did not approve of Emily. His father did not talk to her, and his mother barely acknowledged her. They wanted Emily to sign a pre-nuptial agreement, which was not necessary, I was informed. His inheritance was not community property.

They were married and lived in Atlanta and had two children, Sidney and Ivy. About seventeen years later, Emily divorced Kenneth because he had become an alcoholic.

My daughter Diane graduated from college and went into the military and became a federal agent. She had a tendency to be heavy, and she was very unhappy with her image. She decided to get a lap band, and she lost about 70 pounds, and she is now content. She lives in California and has a lovely group of friends. She is not married. We communicate regularly and see each other as often as possible.

Let's talk about my son, Phillip. He graduated high school and did not want to go to college. I told him that was okay with me, but he would have to move out and get a job. I told him I would only support him while he was in school. He agreed to go to college. He lasted less than a semester. He informed me he was joining the army, but he only stayed in for nine months. He got a general discharge, and came home. I told him he either had to get a job or go back to college. He went back and became an engineer.

He got a job with a national company and surprisingly did very well. The company was bought out by a competitor, who immediately fired most of the employees from the original company. This of course, included Phillip. That was five years ago. He has been unable to get a job. He spends his time gambling, either online or at casinos. I paid his health insurance and rent for two years. I don't do that anymore. We are occasionally in touch with each other.

The final straw with Emily occurred six years ago at a cousin's wedding. Emily got up to make a speech and she proceeded to tell everyone that the bride was like a sister to her and the time spent in their home was the best in her life. That statement ranked among the most hurtful she had ever made. After the wedding when we all went back to the hotel, Emily and I got into a heated discussion, and she told me never to talk to her again.

I did find out that my daughter Emily's therapist told her that if she was unhappy with her mother and couldn't get along with her, she should just cut her out of her life. It seems that this is the new thinking among some therapists. If a relationship is not working, no matter who it is, get rid of it. Perhaps it is wishful thinking, but our relationship might have been saved with a different therapist. Emily's children are now teenagers. Emily and I never talk or communicate with each other.

I am still happily married to Jack. We are celebrating our 26th wedding anniversary.

FOURTEEN

Disloyal and Disrespectful

I grew up in a household where my parents were together, and not together, all of my life. They never should have married, and once they did they should have divorced. I was eight years-old when my father left for the first time, because my mother slapped me. I have a half-sister Pamela, from my mother's previous marriage. Pamela was much older and took care of me like a second mother. We moved from place to place because we had very little money. I spent my childhood pretty much alone, without friends, because of that. My love was for animals and reading.

My father reappeared when I was about eleven. That only lasted about a year. He left again, and we were on the move once more. That is how my parents lived their life together, and apart. My mom worked all those years and managed to keep us together. One day, after many years, we realized my father was never coming back. I finished high school and went to college, thanks to my sister Pamela, who paid for it. I graduated and became a teacher.

I had not met anyone special in all those years. A friend of mine introduced me to her friend, George. We became good friends, and I eventually married him. After about one year, I realized it was not a good situation. I stuck with George because I didn't want to be alone, even though he was not warm, loving, or sexual. We had a friendly relationship. We traveled a good deal.

I told George I wanted to have a baby. I subsequently found out I could not have any children. We then decided to adopt a baby. We waited about one year before our daughter Donna arrived. She was a joy in my life. Less than two years later, we adopted Perry.

Donna started changing her behavior soon after Perry joined our family. As young as she was, she was jealous of Perry, and she carried that through her entire life. Donna was brilliant in school, but not a nice child. She always had a sour face and a sour disposition.

Fast forward to their teenage years. There was constant bickering, and I became their referee. My husband suddenly had a heart attack and died, and about one week later my mother was diagnosed with cancer and moved in with us. From the time my mother moved in to the time of her death, Donna was mean to her grandmother, not helpful, and argumentative. Donna always threatened to leave home at eighteen. Finally, I told her she had to leave, as her behavior was unacceptable. I told her I would find a place for her nearby. She did leave, and I didn't hear from her for a long time. One day, out of the blue, she called and said she was moving to Georgia with her boyfriend, and she did.

Meanwhile, Perry was developing a strong interest in flying. Although we were living on a tight budget since my husband had died, I paid for flying school for Perry. We were very close, and he was appreciative of the support I gave him.

I then received a call from Donna telling me that she had gotten married and had had her wedding at her in-laws' house. She didn't bother inviting me or Perry, her only family. A couple of months later, Donna called to tell me she was expecting a baby. I decided to visit Donna to see where and how she was living. I was in shock when I saw the condition of the "shack" she called home. She had never lived like that before. She gave birth to a little boy, Tom. A few years later she had another baby, Alice.

Meanwhile, Perry graduated from flying school and got a job in the Bahamas. I would visit him every six months, as we enjoyed a warm relationship. Perry then took a job in the States. He always kept in contact with me. Perry met a girl, who he eventually married. He took a job in another state and soon after realized his wife was an alcoholic and was cheating on him. He divorced her.

Donna decided to go back to college. She left the children with her mother-in-law. Through the years, Donna and I fought constantly over everything, most of all about her children being ill-mannered and disrespectful. In spite of our constant disagreements, I paid for her education. Her husband had odd jobs and could barely support the family. When she graduated from college, I invited our friends and family to go to

Georgia and celebrate. We were getting along at that time.

Donna then decided to go for her master's degree. I helped her financially again, even though she never acknowledged my help or showed any gratitude. She graduated and got a job teaching. She divorced her husband and moved into her own place with her daughter Alice. Her son Tom moved in with his dad.

I got very sick with a degenerative cervical problem. I refused to have surgery. Instead I was given a number of medications that caused me to be mentally and physically unable to do anything. My friend called Donna and asked her to come get me and take me home to Georgia. She did.

When we got to her place, she put me into a room that had been my grandson's. It was filthy and crammed with "stuff", leaving me with very little room. Donna went to work and left me alone. I had severe anxiety and panic attacks. My granddaughter Alice was in high school and going out at night. Donna had a boyfriend. Two nights a week she would sleep with her boyfriend at his house and leave me alone. She was very mean to me.

One night she came home, packed my things and drove me to a mental hospital. The doctor refused to accept me and told Donna to take me home. She was furious. The next day she found a retirement place to dump me into. I decided I would get better by myself so I could go home. I did, and I drove myself home and continued my recovery. I went to a chiropractor who gave me laser treatments, and I am now in great shape without any surgery or pills.

Back to Perry. He moved to Washington and shortly thereafter met a young Asian girl, Yetta. He called to tell me he planned to marry Yetta, and he invited me to their wedding. They subsequently moved to Colorado. As I was planning a vacation, I called Perry to say I would be travelling near him. I wanted to stay over for a few days before continuing my vacation. I did visit, and we had a misunderstanding about something said to me by Yetta's mother. It got heated, and I left.

They had a baby girl. I offered to visit with them to help take care of the baby. Perry told me he didn't need me to visit as he was taking time off to help out. A few days later I called to see how everyone was, and I was told Yetta's Mom was there to help.

About a year after the baby was born, Perry called to tell me he was flying into a town near me. I met him, and we hugged and hugged, and talked about the baby. I had not yet seen the baby. I called Perry a few months later and told him about another vacation I was planning. I told him I wanted to see the family and especially the baby. He told me I was no longer welcome in his home. This statement came as a complete shock, especially since our previous meeting was so loving. When I questioned him as to the reason for his attitude, he refused to discuss it. He then hung up on me. That was seventeen years ago.

After I realized I was not going to ever hear from him again, my heart was breaking, and I was in pain. I sought out a therapist. I went for three years until I could function again without Perry in my life. I expected that behavior from Donna, but not Perry. Because we were so close, I expected

Perry to tell his wife, who didn't like me at all, that he wanted a relationship with me, and that she did not have to have one with me. But he never did.

I had to have heart surgery. Donna knew about it and was too busy to be at my side. When she finally called, I told her I didn't want her as my daughter anymore because she was mean, uncaring, disloyal and disrespectful. I told her, "We are over."

I am back to teaching and doing well physically and emotionally. I am in the process of taking baby steps towards making a new life for myself, without my children.

FIFTEEN

Too Many Apologies

Barry and I have been married 58 years. We have two daughters, Fran 53 and Hilda 51. We have been estranged from Hilda for about 12 years, but are close to our older daughter, Fran. I hate using that word "Estranged," but that's what it is. My children had a normal childhood and got along with each other. Then came the teenage years, and Hilda started to change. I thought the change was because of the friends she was seeing. She started to have problems, so we took her to Jewish Family Services. After we all met we were told we had a normal family unit, but perhaps Hilda might benefit from therapy.

Hilda was becoming obstinate and doing only what she wanted to do, no matter what we suggested. Against our wishes, she decided to leave school at 16 years of age. We met with her guidance counselor, who thought Hilda was very bright and personable. But Hilda was lazy and not interested in continuing her education. She left school and continued living at home. She did take a GED and passed with high marks. We told her to go back to school, or get a job, or leave our house. She went to beauty school but did not get her license. She went to college and got good marks, but she never finished her schooling.

Our older daughter Fran went to college and graduated with honors. Hilda then went to the same college as Fran, but didn't like it, so she came home and went to a community college. She finally abandoned college altogether. Hilda then went to work in different industries and could not hold a job for very long. She knew she had to go to school or work at a job in order to live in our home. Since she seemed to be incapable of either, she finally moved out of our house and moved in with friends.

She then met her soon-to-be husband Les, who we liked immediately. He was from Annapolis. She decided after going with Les for a while that she was going to move to Annapolis to be with him. All this time we were all talking to each other and everything was "hunky dory".

About six months after she moved, we got a call from her telling us she was pregnant. We asked if she wanted to keep the baby, and she said, Yes. I suggested that she make me a mother-in-law first, before becoming a grandmother. She agreed to marry Les and asked if we could have a small wedding for them. In two week's time we made all the arrangements, and they married. Les didn't have any family except an aunt and uncle, who we are still close to.

Hilda had the baby. Everything seemed to be fine. She was a stay-at-home mom and would call us every day. Then one day, I suggested that instead of her calling me and spending the money, that I would call her. After that, every time we went to visit she was very snippy. I don't know if it was because of the remark about calling her, but she did seem to change. We would visit on a regular basis, and years went by, but her attitude did not change much.

Then there was the incident with our cat that seemed to change everything. We went to visit them and brought our cat. Their cat had just died, so they were used to having a cat around. Hilda told us we had to keep the cat in our bedroom. My granddaughter, Sara, who was then six years-old, came into the room. She asked to pet the cat, which we said was okay. But, if you are petting a cat and stop, some cats will snip at you. It's their way of telling you not to stop petting.

Of course, our granddaughter got frightened and started to cry when the cat snipped at her. We hugged and kissed her to make her feel better. My daughter then came along and wanted to know what we had done to Sara to make her cry. She didn't see our hugging and kissing each other. She accused us of mistreating Sara, just as we had mistreated her. (We always felt like we had to walk on eggshells with Hilda.)

We were very uncomfortable with Hilda, but not so with Les, our son-in-law. The calls stopped after the cat incident. There was no contact, except when I would call them. Most of the time I had to leave a message.

Hilda and Les would have Passover dinners at a hotel. We were never invited, but my daughter Fran and her family were invited. I told Fran that Passover was eight days, and if she chose to, she could divide her time between her sister and us. That is what she finally did. We would make Thanksgiving dinner, and we always invited our children. Fran would attend, but Hilda would not attend or answer our phone calls or emails. Even though it might be hard to believe, Fran claimed she never discussed our problems with Hilda.

One of Hilda friends, who kept in touch with us, told us she had asked Hilda about the problem and Hilda cut her off, and told her not to bring it up again. We asked Les about the problem, and he replied that he didn't think it would ever be resolved, and we never found out the reason. We asked Les's uncle, who was friendly with us, if he knew what was wrong. He told us he didn't know the cause of the problem. He only knew that Hilda was in therapy for a long time. I called Hilda and surprisingly, she answered the telephone. I told her that the only people who could resolve this problem were the two people involved. Hilda told me there was nothing to resolve, and she hung up on me.

Seven years later Hilda gave birth to a son, Zachary. We found out about his birth from my daughter Fran. We never saw this grandchild. We were never advised of his birth. We didn't see Hilda or her family until our daughter Fran's son, Matthew's Bar Mitzvah. We were seated at one table, and Hilda and her family were at another table. I went over to them and kissed Sara, and she was very shy with us. I then went over to our daughter, who was standing by herself, and put my arms around her and kissed her. She never moved a muscle. She stood there like a statue. She showed no affection. I backed off.

There was no communication with us until it was Hilda's daughter's Bat Mitzvah. We were shocked that we were invited, along with Fran's whole family. We held out hope that this would be a new beginning for all of us. The joke was on us. It was a repeat in attitude towards us—coldness to both of us, on Hilda's part.

Five years ago she sent an email demanding that I admit my guilt and apologize. I couldn't do that anymore, because after apologizing one hundred times through the years, I still had no idea what she wanted me to apologize for.

Hilda told Fran that she was having a few problems with Sara, who was 18 years old then. Fran told Hilda that that sounded familiar. She said, "It sounds like the problems you gave Mom when you were a teenager." There has been no

communication with Hilda since we attended
Sara's Bat Mitzvah.

SIXTEEN

Greed

It has been five years since our troubles began. I feel as if I am in a Rod Serling surreal movie, and I can't extricate myself from it.

My husband, Vince and I have been married forty-five years. We were both born and raised in New Jersey. We have two children, our son, Harvey and our daughter, Rita.

I met Vince on a blind date. I didn't like him at first, because he appeared to be too much of a "take charge" person. It grated on my nerves, I guess, because I have a similar type personality. However, Vince was quite persistent in calling me for a date. I thought I could get rid of him faster by agreeing to one date. Much to my surprise, I found him to be intelligent and charming. I realized I had misjudged his previous behavior. We continued dating, and I found myself falling in love with Vince.

We became engaged, but we put our wedding off until we graduated from college. Vince graduated with a degree in business. I went to work for a Special Events company, helping to plan parties in various locations. Vince went to work for his father in the family business, importing porcelain figurines. We were married and settled in a lovely community in New Jersey. It was within easy commuting to Manhattan where the business was located.

When Rita and Harvey were young, Vince and I would take them into Manhattan to visit museums and various children's theatres. And what better way to complete the adventure than to sample the wonderful ethnic foods in New York City. On one of our excursions, we discovered a little bakery specializing in scrumptious cupcakes. They were so delicious we brought some home. This was the beginning of Rita's love-affair with cupcakes. She became interested in learning how to bake them.

We embarked on a baking project, experimenting with producing cupcakes of every color, taste and texture. We laughed our way through all the mistakes we made. During football season, while Vince and Harvey watched the games, Rita and I enjoyed a true mother-daughter bonding, one which I thought could never be broken. Harvey and Rita grew up in a home filled with lots of relatives sharing all the holidays with us, either at our home or theirs. None of these early years prepared us for what was to come.

Our children each married. By this time, Vince was running the family import business almost by himself. My father-in-law had semi-retired. Vince was now ready to take our son, Harvey and our son-in-law, Daniel into our business. Both of them were anxious to begin. After a few years, it became obvious that the boys were well-suited to the business. At this time, Vince decided to make our son Harvey, and our son-in-law Daniel, equal partners, each becoming a vice president in charge of his own division. Our business consisted of two separate corporations — the import of figurines and the sale and marketing of the figurines, both headed by my husband Vince.

As time passed, the business grew, and so did our family. We became proud grandparents. Each of our children had two children of their own. Harvey and his wife, Sonia, had a son Milton, and a daughter, Cindy. Rita and Daniel had a daughter

Melissa and a son, Alec. Each of the children bought a new home to accommodate their growing families. As the family tradition continued, spending as many Sundays as possible at our home, our granddaughters, Melissa and Cindy developed an interest in baking cupcakes too, just as Rita had done.

As the grandchildren grew, so did the special occasions that we attended add up, such as: first birthdays, holiday dinners, graduations from public schools, high school football games, etc. The best part was the extra hugs and kisses we exchanged. Looking back to that time, I would have to say I felt most content with our lives.

One day, my daughter-in-law Sonia came to visit me, and she asked if Daniel was earning more money than Harvey. I told her that they were equal partners. Sonia believed that Daniel and Rita were spending a lot of money on expensive vacations, etc. She couldn't understand how that was possible since she and Harvey couldn't seem to afford those things. I told Sonia that I chalked it up to frugality on the part of my son, her husband Harvey. I didn't think much of it at the time.

Vince decided it was time to sell the import business. Daniel was charged with the responsibility of getting the books in order to show the prospective buyers. Harvey was charged with getting the inventory and orders completed. While all these preparations were happening, our bookkeeper came to Vince, quite troubled. There were a number of checks she could not find an explanation for. The prospective buyers found some irregularities that could not be explained. Vince, along with our accountant, called a family meeting.

It became clear that Daniel was writing a check from one corporation to another and then to himself. In the beginning, I had a hard time saying this—Daniel was stealing thousands of dollars from us. The worst part, if there is a worse part, is that our daughter Rita knew about it. How could our daughter sanction this thievery? Needless to say, the sale of the import business was cancelled.

We had a meeting with Daniel and Rita and made them a monetary offer to leave the business. Not only did Daniel and Rita not accept what we thought was a fair offer, but they refused all offers, and they took us to court to retain part of the business. After a few years of court battles, we came to an agreement, which among other requirements, removed Daniel from the business permanently. We all let out a big sigh of relief and hoped the unpleasantness was finally behind us. We no longer have any contact with Rita or her children, our grandchildren.

We wonder if Rita realizes that the inheritance she would have gotten has been spent on all the legal matters.

It is very sad that the family is broken because of their greed. There is a terrible emptiness in our life without Rita and her family.

SEVENTEEN

Enough is Enough

My husband Lew and I have been married 49 years. I was seventeen when I got married. My husband was twenty-five. We had a blind date set up by our families. We had one date, and he proposed to me. Lew said it was love at first sight for him. He was in the navy and had to go back to Pensacola. He said he didn't want me going off to college where I would meet other men. He promised to send me to college if I married him right away. I was swept off my feet by his sudden proposal, and I agreed to marry him.

When I finished my four years of college, and he finished his time with the navy, we went to Washington D.C. He returned to his job as a physicist for the Department of the Army. I went back to school and got a degree in instrumental music and voice education. I became a Cantor and played the guitar.

We had our first son, Arthur, about a year after I started working. Lew and Arthur were very close as Arthur grew up. They became best friends. About 3 ½ years later we had our second son, Ron. We never had any financial help from anyone, even during the four years I went to college. We bought a house near where Lew was going to be working. We always looked to the future to choose what path we needed to take.

We became very active in a synagogue, and as Arthur grew he too became involved with the youth groups. He was very math oriented, and very bright. Arthur was really into Judaism. We were very close. Ron was just the opposite. I was not close to Ron at that time. He was his own person. I taught Arthur to play the flute when he was in fourth grade. He continued to play the flute in every school band throughout his years. I would have to say my husband and I were both closer to Arthur than to Ron. But as time went on, I realized that Ron could teach us in different ways.

Arthur and I were not into sports. Ron was big into sports, and eventually I started to learn more about it, and I had enjoyable times with Ron, growing closer each time we watched a game together. Ron seemed to be a little jealous of

Arthur because Arthur was allowed to do things that he was too young to do.

Lew insisted our sons each pick an instrument to play in the band. I knew that children formed bonds with each other with a common interest, like music. Ron chose to play the drums, and Arthur chose the flute. Ron was very smart. One summer he was chosen to be an intern on Capitol Hill, but he did not want to do it. I told him it was a rare opportunity to be chosen, and he would regret it if he turned it down. He eventually agreed and was very happy because he had an opportunity to meet some very famous people. It was a great summer for Ron.

Arthur was finishing his junior year when his professor accused him of cheating on his final exams. Arthur swore to us that he hadn't. We hired an attorney, and of course, Arthur was found not guilty. However, during the time it took to examine the circumstances, without telling us, Arthur decided to go to another college because he couldn't deal with the stress. He left us to deal with the college, the trials, etc. This was to become his pattern of behavior. If he couldn't deal with the problem, he would just leave, and we would be stuck to handle the problems.

We eventually bought a house in Florida, and Arthur followed us, buying one for himself. Arthur was still playing the flute professionally. Every time I was hired to play or sing, Arthur accompanied me on the flute.

Arthur started dating and met Mary, who moved in with him, unbeknownst to us. He told us we couldn't come to his house because he was having it painted. He came to visit us after about eight months. He told us he was going to Utah for his business. We were quite surprised. Of course, we later found out it was his way of breaking up with Mary. Arthur hired a real estate agent to rent his home, but he begged us to have the house cleaned and put in shape. This was another irresponsible reaction to not facing the problem of breaking up with Mary. Arthur met another woman, and after a few months they got engaged, but this too did not last.

Then Arthur met Polly, who was not married, but had a six year-old little girl, Karen. Arthur and Polly were a twosome, and before long Polly was pregnant. Arthur did not want to marry her because he found her to be mean and vindictive, and she did not want an abortion. Polly decided that she did not want Arthur talking to us. For eight months we did not hear from him. Arthur was living in Polly's house. Polly said, "If you love me, you will not talk to your parents, because I need you more than they do."

Polly gave birth to a baby girl, Robin. After Robin was born, we made up with Arthur. Arthur stayed with Polly about three months before leaving her. He always paid child support. Arthur was able to get visitation rights to see Robin. We got very attached to Robin and were a regular in her life and enjoyed many special occasions together.

We became friendly with a family in our community. They happened to have a single daughter, Iris, and we happened to have our son, Arthur nearby. We introduced them, and Iris seemed taken with Arthur. After two months they got engaged, and she moved in with Arthur. Everything was quite pleasant. She accepted Robin, and we all saw each other on a regular basis. We spoke to Arthur and told him we were concerned that he might do the same thing again—stop talking to us. He assured us that would not happen. Iris decided to become a vegan, and she was upset that Arthur didn't. After that, for no apparent reason, Iris decided that Arthur and Robin could not visit with us.

Arthur no longer has any communication with us. We had one of Arthur's friends intercede for us. We were told if we wrote an email this would help "bury the hatchet". We wrote it, but never received a response. It was like a faucet—turn it on—turn it off. Ron, in all of this, did not want to have anything to do with Arthur and his family.

Iris got pregnant and convinced Arthur that they had to move away. They moved to California. We did not know this was happening. Iris's brother warned us that she was mentally ill, and at first we found that hard to believe. Arthur put his house on the market and sold it. They had a child that we never saw, and we never heard from them. Arthur only saw Robin once or twice a year, as she was living with her mom.

Sometime later, we were presented with a letter accusing Lew of molesting Robin. We were in shock. Polly called the Rabbi of the Synagogue where Lew was teaching and informed him of the pending case. Of course, Lew was fired. We were investigated and found not guilty. At the trial our son Arthur testified that everything in the letter was true and that his father was guilty.

We reached a point where we felt that we could no longer put up with the abuse, and that it wasn't worth the few minutes we were allowed to see Robin. Once we reached this conclusion, it made us stronger to deal with the loss. The loss of our son Arthur is irreparable. We ripped up his birth certificate, and all his pictures. It is as if he never existed. Any son who would accuse my husband, his father, of being a child molester can never be forgiven. We can never go back. You need to know when enough is enough. When you know that, it becomes easier to get on with one's life.

EIGHTEEN

Replacement Mom

My name is Lili, and I was born in Brooklyn. I met my husband Josh while still a teenager. We fell in love instantly and were able to marry quickly since Josh was a practicing accountant in the garment industry. Five years later we had our first daughter, Sharon, two years later our second daughter Lucille, and a few years after her, our youngest daughter Wendy was born.

I knew for a fact that organized crime took over the garment industry. My husband began to do very well financially as he got more involved with them. He became the front for them in their legitimate garment industry businesses. He would meet with them on Friday nights for coffee. Little did I know that it was more than coffee. There were women involved too. He kept this up for years, but it must have been bothering him because eventually he had a nervous breakdown.

During this time, our youngest daughter Wendy ran away from home at the age of 14. I subsequently found out that Wendy had stolen money from her father's wallet, which gave her the wherewithal to run away. I gave the police pictures of Wendy, and they sent the photos to all the police agencies across the United States. About one month later we received a call from the police in Los Angeles. They found her sleeping in the street. I sent money to the police, so they could put her on a bus for home.

When Wendy arrived home, I noticed she was losing her hair. She didn't seem to know who she was, and she couldn't find herself. I started taking her to doctors to find the cause of her hair loss. We finally went to a dermatologist, who immediately told us that she was pulling her own hair out. The doctor believed she had 'impulse control disorder' which was often chronic. Wendy ran out of the office crying. When we got home I tried talking to her. She insisted it was my fault, but she could not or would not tell me exactly what my fault was. She never stopped pulling her hair out and ended up wearing expensive wigs for the rest of her life.

I took Wendy to a number of therapists, all of whom were unacceptable to her. Finally, she found a therapist she felt comfortable with.

However, she formed a friendship with him and his wife. They became so personally involved that they were really not able to help her. She finished high school and went to the school of Art and Design, but dropped out. She ran away from home at about the age of 18, and married a boy that was going into the army. At that point I had no connection with her whatsoever.

I found it curious, that while Wendy lived with us, she was never affected by her father's nervous breakdown, while our other two daughters were greatly affected by it. However, they had their own lives. Both were out of the house by then. Sharon had married and has two wonderful kids. Lucille never married.

I began entertaining the idea of divorcing Josh, as his behavior was quite erratic. A friend of mine told me of a new anti-depressant that had just been discovered at Rockland State Hospital. I immediately made an appointment to see a physician, who believed my husband was a candidate for this new treatment, and we were able to get the medication. We were informed that it would take at least three weeks for it to take effect, and it did. He was back working again and behaving like the man I married. Our marriage was perfectly normal. This lasted about six years, and then he informed me that he was going off his medication.

It took only three more weeks when he informed me that he wanted no part of me. He wouldn't talk to me, look at me, or have sex with me. He blamed me for the way he was feeling. He thought he was cured and didn't have to take the medicine. He also liked the fast lifestyle again. He was hanging out with the "Mafia" boys. He went up to the Catskills for a vacation and met a woman he had known before, and who I found out later had been a prostitute years earlier. I started divorce proceedings, and Josh moved in with his new girlfriend.

My dear girlfriend died, and her husband Sam, whom I had known for over twenty-five years, started visiting me. Eventually, he became my constant companion.

By this time, Wendy had two children. Her husband was not working, and he had girlfriends. He became abusive and threw Wendy down a flight of stairs. I had had no contact with Wendy for years, but when she called to tell me what happened, I went to her rescue. I told her she had to divorce her husband because it was becoming dangerous for her and the children. I began giving her money.

My ex-husband was paying her rent so they could all survive. I went to visit Wendy and the children and found her apartment to be full of bugs. I couldn't believe how dirty the place was. I told Wendy she had to move because it was not healthy to live in that environment and that I would help her. She immediately summoned my grandsons and told them how mean I was. She had never told them I was paying a large percent of her bills. My grandson screamed at me to leave the house and never come back, and I didn't.

Sam and I moved to Florida. I moved in with him until I could find my own home, which I did. Wendy eventually called and said she wanted a relationship. She even visited me in Florida. However, she told my grandsons all about her childhood and that everything that went wrong was my fault. My grandsons were very distant, and it became obvious that they blamed me for everything. I never saw them again. They married and had children. I never saw my great-grandchildren.

My daughters, Sharon and Lucille, decided to make me an 80th birthday party, and they talked Wendy into participating. We were all looking forward to a family reunion. I had taken $400.00 out of the bank for incidentals. Sharon, Lucille and I decided to go to the gym. Upon our return home, I found that the cash was missing from my wallet and Sharon's driver's license was also missing. We could not figure out what had happened.

The next day Wendy said that she was leaving and would not stay for the party. We could not talk her into staying. At that time, Wendy told me she did not want me as her mother. She said she'd found a replacement for me. That was the last time I ever saw or heard from Wendy. In the meantime, Sharon had to file for a new driver's license and all that it entailed. She was very upset.

About one year later I had to go for some medical tests. I wanted a small purse. I went into the back of my closet and found one I had not used in a while. Upon opening it, I found my daughter's driver's license in it. Sharon was very angry with

Wendy. There was no reason for Wendy to have done that. Wendy was always jealous of Sharon, even though Sharon gave her money and jewelry. It was never enough. She also paid for Wendy's wig which was $2,000.00. I finally realized that I didn't want Wendy in my life anymore either.

Going back in time, when Wendy was seven years old, she brought home Myrna, a friend living on the same street. Myrna lived with her grandmother, who was on Medicaid. Her mother was a drug addict and could not care for her. She didn't have many clothes and probably didn't eat right. Our home became her second home. I didn't know it at the time, but Wendy was stealing cash from my husband's wallet and buying herself and Myrna all kinds of goodies.

At that time we lived in a very upscale neighborhood. Our house was quite large and very impressive. We never were in need of anything material and shared our good fortune with Myrna. We made her feel very much a part of our family.

Seven years ago, Myrna found Wendy on Facebook. She wanted to know how to contact me.

Wendy would not tell her my whereabouts, and she told Myrna to never contact her again. She also told her to stay away from me. Wendy wrote her a very nasty letter. In spite of that, Myrna would not give up, and she finally found Sharon and Lucille on Facebook. My daughters felt like they had found their little sister.

When Myrna found me, she was living in Alabama with her husband and son. She asked if they could all come for a visit, and I was thrilled that she had such fond memories of her childhood with me. Soon after their visit with me, Myrna called to tell me that they had decided to move to Florida to be near me.

God works in strange ways. My daughter Wendy found a replacement for me, and I found a replacement for her. Myrna and her husband take a deep interest in me. I am very lucky. I am very happy. I have my boyfriend, my daughters and a good life. At the age of 85, I am in a show where I am singing and dancing. My life is wonderful.

Dr. David R. Miller earned his Ph.D. in educational psychology and counseling from the University of South Carolina and is an author of several books. When Dr. Miller learned about this book, he offered the following story for inclusion. I thought it might add a different perspective to these stories.

NINETEEN

Rules of Estrangement

Joan and Allen were a fifty-something couple with a professional appearance and matching mannerisms. They met and married while students at a large Midwestern university. They had been married for almost thirty years when I met them in the counseling office at the hospital where I worked as a child/adolescent/family therapist. They had a good marriage, according to them, but they were not in my office to talk about themselves.

Joan and Allen had not been able to have children and so, after exhausting all other avenues, they decided to adopt. After examining adoption, with all the corresponding opportunities and obstacles, they decided to arrange to adopt two very young girls who were at that time living in an orphanage just outside Seoul, South Korea. They had learned about the orphanage through missionaries at their church, who had served there for a time.

Fast forward 20 years. The girls had been raised in the same Midwestern city where their adoptive parents attended university and where the younger daughter was now a student. The older had already graduated and moved to a city in a neighboring state for her work. These girls were very smart, highest grades for both all through their school years, each enjoying a scholarship because of such good grades. The girls were, to use their parents' description, "brilliant and not a spot of trouble".

So why the counseling appointment? Good marriage, great kids, mom, dad, and daughters clearly high-achieving and well-motivated people. What could be wrong with this picture? With much hesitation and glances at each other, they began to unfold their story.

These adoptive parents told me that they felt their daughters were "cutting them off". While they were supporting the younger daughter, who was still in college, they sensed that she was beginning to show the same behavior as her older sister, that is, distancing themselves from parents.

The counseling session I am discussing occurred mid March. The older daughter had not come home for Christmas, claiming that her work would keep her too busy to travel the 100 or so miles to come home. The younger daughter told them that this year, if they didn't mind too much, she would spend Christmas at her sister's apartment so she wouldn't be alone for the holidays. This was the first time the family had not been together for the holidays.

When Joan suggested that they might travel to be with them at the apartment, the older sister claimed it would be too crowded. Joan and Allen commented that they had noticed that their daughters had not sent birthday or Christmas cards during the previous year, as well. The Christmas gifts Joan and Allen sent their daughters were accepted but no thanks were forthcoming and no gifts were sent from daughters to parents that year. These parents were seriously hurt by what was happening to their family.

Through the course of several counseling sessions we explored the potential reasons for the changes these parents were seeing. The idea of estrangement was brought up and led the three of us to some issues that, while still painful, helped lessen the worry and anxiety they were experiencing. What follows is a synopsis of our discussions over several sessions.

To begin, we decided it was important to recognize the issue of adoption. Even though too young to remember their life in South Korea, the girls, who obviously looked different from their parents, were gently told what little was known about their early life and the circumstances of their adoption. It was significant that the girls had been discussing a return visit to South Korea, not to live, but to explore their roots. Joan and Allen had been in favor of the trip.

It is a sad reality that many adopted people, of whatever age, never make the necessary emotional connection to their adoptive parents.

While the girls had been described as loving and respectful, they had never been, to use Joan's terms, "huggy and affectionate". Allen commented that he had been thinking for a long time that the girls might have doubts about the legitimacy of their adoption and the immersion in the American culture. The girls had always expressed a strong interest in their origin, had written papers and done projects on South Korea while in high school, and possessed lots of books on life in South Korea, many of which could still be found in their rooms at home.

Joan and Allen began to understand the issue of estrangement a little better as we moved through the counseling process. They accepted the idea that they were not estranged from their children; the children were estranged from them. These parents wanted nothing more from their girls than to continue to have a relationship with them through life. It was the decision of the daughters to reduce and eventually eliminate family contact, which is what happened. But Joan and Allen were helped just a little by the recognition that this was not of their doing and had, in retrospect, been developing in their children for many years.

Their daughters simply, if for unknown reasons, decided that, while they were thankful for the upbringing they had received from their adoptive parents, it was now time to say, "Thanks, and we'll see you later." We may never know why these girls decided to eliminate their adoptive parents from their lives, but this is what they did. In many other situations, not only involving adoption, we see the same thing happening.

Estrangement from parents without cause is impossible to satisfactorily explain. Children, who have not been abused or mistreated in other ways, sometimes choose to make enemies of their parents and just leave without further contact. When this kind of tragedy happens, it is crucial that the parents understand that it is not they who have made the decision. It is not they who bear the responsibility for this disruption in family interaction, and while it is no less painful for the parents, pain with no responsibility for causing the pain is easier to bear.

Why do some of our grown children decide to separate themselves from us and, often, the rest of the family? I suggest the cause has more to do with personality formation than anything else, personality formation that no parents can control as much as we might wish. I have had adults tell me that they decided to distance themselves from their parents just because they didn't "like" a parent or parents. Sometimes they felt unloved and less favored, which may or may not be true, who can tell with something as deeply seated as this?

If you or someone you know is dealing with being cut off from contact by a grown child, please recognize the reality that the responsibility, except for cases of mistreatment, of course, rests with the grown child. Recognize that while we parents have great responsibility for raising our children, some of us will grow a child who genuinely cannot tolerate being in the presence of his or her parents. We must accept the next step that when children choose to become "estranged" from their parents, they alone bear the responsibility for failing to honor and respect their parents, and they alone have the power to make things right again.

What should parents whose children have estranged themselves from them do?

Continue the contact as much as you are able. Continue to send Christmas cards and birthday cards, check enclosed, even if the checks are never cashed. Consider this an investment in possible future reconciliation. Keep your estranged children informed of family changes, weddings and funerals, for example, even if they do not respond. We want to keep the channels of communication open if at all possible. If praying is part of your life-view, then pray for your 'distanced' child.

How do we conclude such a difficult topic? I wish I could be more optimistic, but I have always been a "glass-half-empty" kind of guy. Just remember, this was not your fault, and you can't fix it on your own.

Life has knocked me down a few times.
It has shown me things I never wanted
          to see.
I have experienced sadness and failure
But one thing is for sure, I always get up.
                              --unknown

About the Author

June Ann Elston

June and her husband Roger live in Wellington, FL with their dog "Sunshine".

47604175R00104

Made in the USA
San Bernardino, CA
04 April 2017